A BOOK FOR AMAIA:

A GRANDFATHER'S ATTEMPT TO BRIDGE THE GAP OF TIME

By Roberto Guzmán-Sosa

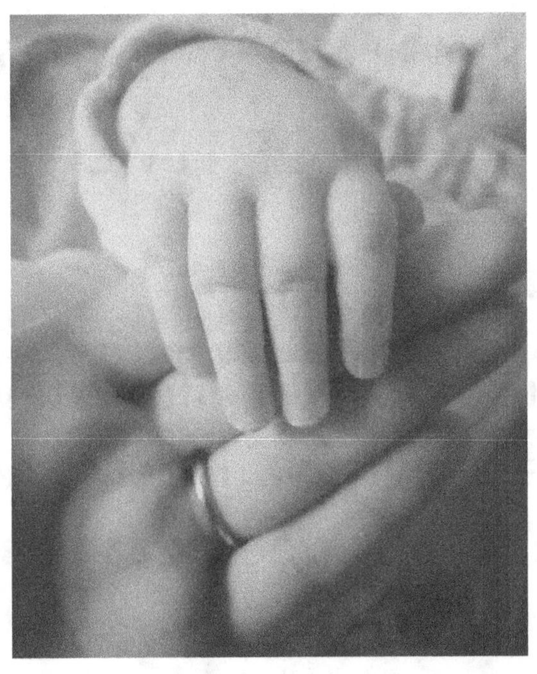

Editorial Libélula Azul

2019

A BOOK FOR AMAIA

A GRANDFATHER'S ATTEMPT TO BRIDGE THE GAP OF TIME

"Thinking about death… produces love for life. When we are familiar with death, we accept each week, each day as a gift. *Only if we are able to accept life bit by bit does it become precious.*"

Albert Schweitzer

ROBERTO GUZMÁN-SOSA

Editorial Libélula Azúl

2019

First Edition

Edición a cargo de La Casa Editora de Puerto Rico,
PO Box 1393, Río Grande, Puerto Rico, 00745.
lustrodegloria@gmail.com, www.lacasaeditoradepuertorico.org Tel.
(787)550-3666.

Dedication

This book is dedicated to all the little people being born around the world every single day. May we adults do everything within our power to make the world a better place for *all* of them, for as someone once so wisely said, *"We do not inherit the Earth from our parents, we borrow it from our children."*

ISBN: 9781729068199

Contents

An Introduction for my 'Unintended' Audience

When I started writing this book for my granddaughter it was meant to be only for her. A written tribute to a beautiful, small human being that had just joined our family. *Mi primera nieta*, my first granddaughter.

Just a few days after her birth in Puerto Rico, at a moment when life seemed especially good, my son and I had just finished lunch at home when I felt a strong burning pain in my chest. At first I thought it was heartburn due to a somewhat spicy meal. Puerto Rican food much like Mexican food can sometimes pack a kick in the spices department. However when my left arm became numb I realized it was far more serious. I was having a heart attack. I remained calm. There was a good hospital a fifteen minute drive away. I would get there as quickly as I could.

I managed to drive from our home to the hospital with my son in the passenger seat of my pickup truck. It was only a short drive but that day it felt so much longer than fifteen minutes. I was sweating profusely, hand eye coordination was becoming slower and my reactions were a bit sluggish.

Perhaps driving myself to the hospital was not the smartest thing I had ever done. Anyhow we made it safely to the ER. But the experience for me was, pun intended, somewhat heart breaking. I had two major heart arteries clogged and I needed them cleared. After nearly 8 days and two catheterisms my heart was repaired and I was sent back home a changed man.

Nothing would ever be the same. After that experience I realized in a very new way how amazingly fragile life is. I knew this before but not as I knew it now. I had so much to look forward to. I had a beautiful new granddaughter and I had my lovely daughter who was growing into motherhood in a wonderful way. She was working so hard in her new role and it was something to see. I felt so much pride because of them. I also had my son and the rest of my very imperfect but loving family and friends.

I wanted to live for as long as I could. I *needed* to be a part of their lives. Yet I knew that I had no reason to be sure that that would ever happen. All it would take was for my ticker to stop ticking and as Porky Pig would say at the end of every Merrie Melodies cartoon of my childhood *"That's all Folks!"*

There was so much I wanted to do, to share, to live with my family, especially our new little one. As a writer there was only one way I could, to a point, cheat death. I could write a book for her. So that's what I did.

When I shared this idea with a few close friends they not only liked it, some said that I should make the book available to other people, other parents or grandparents that perhaps wanted to leave something for their own little ones. They argued that not everyone had the time or perhaps the ability to put in printed words all the wonderful things that exist in their hearts and minds, things they need to say before they moved on to the undiscovered country.

Apart from writing the book itself I had two other challenges. The first one was the language. Even though Spanish is and always will be a major component of our identity as Puerto Ricans I decided to write in English because my granddaughter was living in the United States. However even if she eventually lives in Puerto Rico I hope she grows up to be fully bilingual. Both Spanish and English should be part of her cultural heritage. There will be essays on Puerto Rico's language and culture towards the end of the book.

The second issue was the level of complexity and sophistication of the book itself. Again I hope that she will soon learn how to speak and read English well enough to slowly understand all the things I want to share with her here.

Vocabulary is to language what Lego blocks are to building plastic structures. She will need to gather and understand a good amount of words before she can build true and deep understanding of ideas and concepts. I hope she does so early in life. While I tried to simplify the language I did not water down the content of the book. With time my dear granddaughter will hopefully rise to the challenge that I am presenting in the book I've written for her. Finally, there is no reason she needs to read any of this all alone or all at once. Other loved ones may sit down with her and read it for her or with her.

While not originally intended for others, perhaps there is something in her book that can help other families bridge both time and space and leave some thoughts for those who will live in the house of tomorrow, a house us older folks may never visit.

However, love and the printed word can allow me and you to visit the house of tomorrow in a way no other thing can ever do. So sit back and read my attempt at remaining a small part of my granddaughter's life even after my heart has stopped beating and I become simply a memory and a few photographs. Maybe others will find some things here they can share with their own loved ones.

Who knows? Perhaps these words will inspire others to write their own books for all those other beautiful Amaias all over the world. No need to wait for a health crisis to get started.

Roberto Guzmán-Sosa

Aguadilla, Puerto Rico

December 19, 2017

An Introduction for my new granddaughter

When your grandfather wrote these words he was 57 years of age. You were a little over six months old, our new baby. He wrote them because he felt there was so much he wanted to share with you and he wasn't sure if he was going to be around long enough to actually be there by your side. The Guzmán family has a very bad history of heart problems and your granddad suffered a heart attack just days after you were born. He spent eight days in the hospital and he learned a lot about how fragile life really is. Nearly all his uncles, four in total, had died of massive, unexpected heart attacks. Still your *abuelo* wasn't going to let a little thing like death stop him from speaking to you, his lovely granddaughter.

You see Amaia, your *abuelo* was a writer and he realized that he could 'cheat' death thru the magic of *his writing* and *wonder of your reading*. He could still get in touch with you no matter what the Grim Reaper did. So that's the very first thing he wants you to understand, *reading and writing are almost magical things.* When you pick up a good book you can listen to the voice of people across time and space. You can visit other worlds, places and cultures. You can feel the writer's happiness or pain. Her dreams and hopes are all there for you to share and understand.

So your *abuelo* decided to write some things that he hoped would make your life a little bit better. Take what you need and leave the rest. Perhaps in time you'll find better ideas.

These words you see here are born of his love for you, his little one. You may never know how much your coming into our lives meant to all of us. The love that your mom, Jenny showered you with was impressive. Your grandparents on both sides of the family were just amazed by your presence. You were a little piece of humanity that filled our lives with light, pride and hope. Your lovely smile and your big expressive eyes enchanted us all. You helped bring us all together as a family and helped us find new meaning in life.

Yet *abuelo* must warn you. *Life is not always easy and things change.* Sometimes they change for the better but sometimes for the worse. In your life there will be good days, sunny, lovely days. These will be the days you wish would last forever. But they won't, so enjoy them.

There will also be hard days, sad days, dark days. Don't lose your faith because these won't last forever either. Everybody has both kinds of days, everybody. This is *completely normal* my dear, so enjoy the good ones and be as strong as you can during the other ones. What your *abuelo* is going to share with you here will help you get more out of the good days and hopefully give you some strength to face the bad ones.

Your book is divided into some topics that are, in your granddad's opinion, very important. Each essay will briefly discuss what your grandfather learned about life in his brief stay on this little blue planet. Don't you think, however, that your grandfather was some kind of wise old man like Obi Wan Kenobi, the old sage from the Star Wars movies. He wasn't.

Your grandfather was a very imperfect man who tried to learn from his many mistakes. And just so you know, he did make mistakes, *a lot* of mistakes, some small others big. This book is an attempt to help you avoid some of these errors. This may save you from a lot of suffering and pain.

This book is also your grandfather's effort to make up for some of the harm done thru his negligence and immaturity to those before you, a way of saying he's sorry and he wants to make amends. As you will surely learn, in life *no apology is complete without an effort to fix* as best as you can *what has been broken.*

One thing you must always remember is that to a great degree this thing called *life is whatever YOU want it to be.* You have the awesome power of choice. Most of the things that happen to people, good and bad, are usually the result of the decisions they make. So be very, very careful when making decisions. A very smart writer once said that *we are masters of our choices but slaves to their consequences.*

This is very true. Throughout your life you will be making all kinds of choices so *choose wisely.* Take the time to think carefully about the things you are planning to do. Seek advice from people you trust and care about you. Do not rush into anything. Try to imagine what will happen once the choice has been made. Look at the results of the decisions made by others in similar situations. Use your imagination.

This is important because once you set things into motion it is sometimes very difficult to stop the consequences. However you should *never be a victim.* Victims put themselves under the control of others and that is never a good idea. You are not powerless. You are strong and powerful when you take the time to think *before* you act.

Be a fighter. Be strong, independent and smart. Define yourself. *Never allow others to tell you who you are.* You are unique. *Don't you ever forget that.* Do not let anyone put you down or make you feel like you are less than what you are. You are not alone. *Surround yourself with people of good quality* because as the Beatles once sang we all need 'a little help from our friends' to live a happy life. More on this later.

This thing called life is a beautiful mystery for you to enjoy with those you love and in turn love you. I hope you have a long, beautiful life surrounded by people who love, respect and support you always. *Un abrazo para mi amada Rabbitinita.* Let's get started.

About Life and Learning:

"Learn from yesterday, live for today, hope for tomorrow."

Albert Einstein

Even before you were born you were already learning. When you were inside your mom you could hear her voice, her heartbeat and you could even taste the food she enjoyed. When you finally saw the light of day you were like a beautiful little scientist absorbing everything that was happening around you. You made funny sounds and funny faces while playing with your mom. *Learning is a big, big part of a happy life and even as a baby you knew it.*

Some learning happens automatically. You learned to sit up, to crawl, stand up and slowly you learned how to walk and finally run. *Never stop learning* Amaia and *never stop asking questions and you will never stop growing*. As a baby you were pretty easy to entertain. I would go out and carry you around the neighborhood. Whenever you got restless I would look for something interesting, a leaf, a shiny toy, an object with an interesting shape or texture and I would give it to you. That's all it would take. You would study the leaf carefully, turn it around in your little hands and even smell it or try to taste it.

Of course, we would all be very careful not to let you 'taste' anything dangerous but it was so beautiful to see you exploring and discovering the things around you. *You were a little researcher, making experiments and exploring your world.* But learning isn't always a pleasant thing. Sometimes it can be uncomfortable.

Once I gave you a leaf without noticing that it had a couple of fire ants. They bit you and you cried. Not a pleasant experience and for a while you stopped 'trusting' leaves.

When things don't work out you can still learn from that bad experience. Sometimes learning what NOT to do is a very important lesson. Pain, physical and even emotional pain, is the way life warns us to *move away* from some activities, places or even people. *Always listen to what an experience is telling you.* Someone once said something both funny and generally true. *Everybody brings happiness to our lives. Some when they arrive and others when they leave.* Letting go of some things and some people can be just as important as holding on. Letting go can in itself be a great lesson for you.

Not all relationships are good and you need to *be very careful with who you share your time and life with*. There is a very powerful word you should know and use when needed. This is the word NO. If you feel something isn't right for you *do not be afraid to use it*. Say it loud and say it strong. NO.

There are many different ways people learn. They learn from books, they learn by playing and working. You my dear can learn by traveling or doing different things by yourself or with others. You can learn how to ride a bike, build a sand castle or drive a car. Maybe you can learn how to play a piano or a guitar. Some people learn with math, science or literature. Find things you like and learn, learn and learn.

Also learn how to do things you *don't* like. For example, doing the laundry, cleaning and organizing you home or cooking a meal may not be the most exciting things in the world for most people but they are *life skills*. Learn how to do them well for you will be doing them for the rest of your life.

Remember that the best learning is achieved by DOING things not just watching others. Try to do something new every single day of your life. Take in the fresh air of a brand new morning and be grateful for all the wonderful things there are for you to enjoy, for you to learn.

A warning about questions. Some people don't like questions. They will try to stop you from asking them. Be very careful with this kind of people. They may even try to put you down by trying to intimidate you or make you feel bad. They may question your reasons for asking, your motives. If someone does not answer your questions to your satisfaction look for answers elsewhere. For in life it is much better to have questions that cannot be answered than to have answers that cannot be questioned.

Never let anyone kill your curiosity. You cannot learn if you do not feed your mind and heart with good information from good sources. Good sources may include smart, good people you trust, good books, videos, all kinds of experts in different areas of knowledge. Amaia, you have been born in an age of information. It is easy to gather good information using the Internet. In this time and age there is no excuse for being ignorant, for not knowing.

Do you want to fix something? Do you want to cook the perfect mofongo? Check out YouTube. Do you want to know if that cell phone you're thinking of buying is a good deal? Chances are you can go on line and get a good answer to almost any of these questions. Google, TED.com and Yahoo are all great places to learn new, interesting stuff every day.

However, *never ever confuse knowledge with wisdom*. When a person gathers a lot of information about anything they become knowledgeable, well-informed. That is very good but it's not enough. Wisdom, on the other hand, is much more than just knowing. Wisdom is when you use what you know in a way that makes your life and the life of others better. *Knowing how to safely drive a car is good. Using that skill to go to the right places at the right time is wisdom.*

About Happiness:

"No one can make you happy or give you happiness. Happiness comes from inside you."

Anonymous

Amaia, you were born into a world that has many, many good things. There are so many opportunities to grow and learn but there are also a few very dangerous traps in this modern world. One common mistake that many, many people make is *confusing being with having*. As you grow older you will meet some people that have an obsession with getting things. They want to buy this or buy that. They think that life will be perfect if they could only get that special thing, and *that can be almost anything.* It can be a new phone, a particular gadget, a house, a car or that special dress.

Some very selfish and powerful people will try to make you feel bad or ugly if you don't buy whatever it is they're selling. It's called *marketing* and it can be very harmful. Many marketers will stop at nothing until they persuade you to get their product, but only if you're willing to pay.

They will flood your world with commercials trying to get you to give them your money. Their commercials will try to make you feel that you NEED their products to be happy. Whoever falls into this trap will be in big, big trouble.

There is even a word for this. It's called *consumerism* and it can be a terrible thing. My dear, you are valuable *for who you are not what you have.* If you're a good, strong and decent person you will be good regardless of the price of your clothing or the shoes you wear. Those who think less or more of another person because of the money they have or the car they drive are truly poor people because they really don't know what is truly valuable in life and in others.

On the other hand, a person can have a lot of things and if she's a selfish, superficial fool no amount of money or possessions can change that. There's a funny saying in Spanish, *"Mona aunque se vista de seda mona se queda."* In English it roughly translates, "A chimp dressed in fine silk is still a chimp." Again, remember *we are valuable because of who we are not what we have.*

Having said that, I must acknowledge that there is nothing wrong with having nice things. Having nice clothing, living in a nice home and having other material things is fine. The problem is *when things have you*, when you think that your happiness *depends* on these external objects. That's not how happiness works. *Happiness is not so much about getting what you want as it is about wanting what you have.* Being grateful for all the good we already enjoy is very important in our quest for happiness. As poet Shane Koyczan once wrote, we need to be *savagely grateful* for all the wonderful things and people life has offered us.

It may sound corny, but it really is much better to have peace, love and understanding than to only have things. For anyone to be truly happy they should learn to say bye bye to buy buy.

About Friendship:

"Dear George, no man is a failure who has friends."

Clarence, George Bailey's guardian angel in the classic movie *It's a Wonderful Life.*

This, by the way, is a great old movie. If you haven't seen it, check it out. Now let's talk about friendship.

Having friends, good friends, is a wonderful thing. Friends are like family that we choose ourselves. So be very, very careful who you call a friend. In life most smart people have only a few friends and that is fine. A friend is not something easily found. Good friends are rare and valuable like diamonds. Acquaintances, on the other hand, are plentiful and they are important too but they are not the same as friends. We'll speak about them later.

So, what is a friend? A friend is a person you can trust, a person you feel comfortable with. A friend knows you in a special way and you know her or him. Sometimes friends like the same things you like, the same movies, books, music, dress or food. They may have similar goals and dreams as you do. Or they may be very different from you and that's why you like them. Now friendships, good ones, usually take time to grow. You need to know each other and that usually doesn't happen from one day to another.

Surround yourself with *people of good quality* because they will help you grow. They can actually make you a better person. Bad friends can hurt you in very real and serious ways. If someone isn't good for you just say goodbye and move on. *Life is far too short and valuable to waste it with toxic people.*

Sad to say but some people are like poison. They make you feel bad inside. They add nothing of value to your life yet they can sometimes suck the life out of you. They may put you down and make you feel stupid, inadequate or even bad. Do not allow people, anyone, to use your mind and heart as their garbage can. Let them deal with their trash elsewhere.

Sometimes they will dare you to do this or do that to 'prove' that you are brave or 'prove' that you really love them, whatever. *Do not fall for these false friends.* They are not worth your time or your company. As I said before, say no when you feel it is necessary to say no. Stay away from toxic people. If someone encourages you to lie, cheat, to be rude or to be irresponsible then they do not belong in your life.

This may come as a surprise but knowing what people think isn't as hard as some believe. Just listen to what they say *but only believe what they do.* Their *actions will tell you* what's really in their minds and hearts.

Words are cheap, my dear, but actions are deep. If someone says they will see you at the mall at 2 PM and they show up at 3 that tells you something. Maybe there was a good reason for being late...once or twice. If it happens three or more times then you have a problem because there is *a pattern of neglect,* of negative actions. Always keep your eyes open to patterns, things that happen over and over again. *All the apologies in the world cannot change the fact that you may be dealing with a very irresponsible person who does not really care for you.*

Keep in mind that *excuses are generally very bad things.* They are something we must use when we have failed. So when someone is constantly failing you and coming up with a never ending series of excuses what they are really saying is that you are not that important for them.

Someone once said that *people who are good at making excuses are rarely good at anything else*. Do not accept this kind of conduct from anyone. You deserve better than that and you should demand better than that.

This of course goes both ways. Try not to fail those around you so you won't have to be making excuses all the time and *do not allow* people that are always failing you to be an important part of your life. *Excuses are the nails that build the house of failure.* Do not accept them and try not to make them too often.

There are some things a real friend will never do. Listen up. A friend *will never force you to do something you really don't want to do*. She will know that you have the right to say 'No' and she should not try to make you go against your feelings and values.

A real friend *will never, ever try to separate you from your family*. Some people may try to control you and in order to do this they will try to separate you from those you love, your *familia* or maybe other friends. Never fall into that trap. No one will ever love you more that your family. In good times and bad times we will be there for you.

A true friend however need not agree with you on everything. On the contrary, if a friend sees you doing something dangerous, she will have no trouble telling you what she *really* thinks.

Since we all do dumb things from time to time it's nice to have someone who will warn us of the stupidity of our ways. So don't expect a friend to always agree with all your crazy ideas.

Regarding friendship there's just one more thing I feel is worth mentioning. *To have a friend you must be a friend.* As Laurence the angel said to George Bailey, a person who has good friends is never a truly poor person.

So a real friend is honest, loyal, responsible and loving. She will be there in good times and bad times. Good friends are an extension of your family, never, ever a replacement. If you surround yourself with good people they will help you grow and be happier. We all need good quality people by our side.

Real friends are people that:

- **Respect you** and help you in times of need. You will do the same for them.

As I said before, to have friends you need to be a friend. That is very true. In life we have many acquaintances but not so many friends. True friends *will laugh with you but not at you.*

- **Support you** when you are weak or in trouble. They will be there when others have left.

- **Are honest with you**. They will tell you what you *need* to hear not what you *want* to hear. If friends see you doing something dumb they will tell you even if you don't like it.

- **Will never try to separate from your loved ones** or the things you love. No one in this world will ever love you more than your family. Never let anyone lure you away from your loved ones.

- **Will answer when you call**. If you text or call someone and they regularly ignore your calls that in itself is an answer so don't ignore it. By constantly ignoring you a person is telling you that they're not really interested in you. If that is the case just move on. Amaia, you should *never, ever beg for anyone's time or attention.* Have some dignity. If someone ignores you just let them go and focus on something else.

Before moving on to another topic let's speak a bit about *acquaintances.* These are also very important. They are in fact a big part of most people's lives. These are the medium distance relationships we have with other people in school, at work and in our neighborhoods. They are not as close as friends but they are important nonetheless. When you slowly build these relationships they will help you live your life better. The people who care for us and help us solve our day to day problems, our doctors, our dentists, the person who does your hair, the guy who fixes your car, good teachers, they are all very important. We should pay attention to them, respect them and reward them by keeping our word when we promise to meet them or pay for their services as needed.

With time you will have many acquaintances and that is a very good thing. Care for them and allow them to grow. Maybe some of them will eventually become your friends. All good relationships need to be taken care of. If you ignore them long enough relationships, like house plants, will die and you will have to start all over again. Not a smart thing to do.

About Luck and Hard Work:

"I think the harder you work the more luck you'll have."

Dave Thomas founder of Wendy's restaurants

"When it comes to luck, you make your own."

Bruce Springsteen, rock star

Some people speak about having good luck or bad luck. They believe that if things go well then it's because they are lucky. If things do not go their way then they feel that they must be victims of bad luck. Most of the time this is not true. A very wise man called Seneca once said that luck is when *preparation meets opportunity.* I think this man, who lived more than 2000 years ago, got it right.

If you work hard and *smart* you will be able to take advantage of the opportunities that come your way. *There are no shortcuts my dear.* If you want to be good at anything you need to put in the time and the effort. This is how someone put it. You must *do today* what others do not want to do, so you can do *tomorrow* what others cannot do. Practice, practice and when you're finished and tired practice some more. You need to *believe in yourself* even when others don't and you must work hard when others aren't even looking. If you want to make your dreams come true *you must be driven*.

As you get better at something you will become more confident and you'll see that *what you need to succeed is inside you* not outside. The study of how people become successful is pretty interesting.

One of my favorite books on this topic is *Outliers* by Malcolm Gladwell. Gladwell studied successful people and he found that they had some things in common. They practiced their craft intensely. When others were playing, video gaming or relaxing they were doing what they loved to do over and over again.

Some people call this a *work ethic* and it seems to apply equally well to individuals, cities or even whole countries. Those who are willing to put in the time and surround themselves with others that have similar goals and dreams are more likely to make good things happen.

They also tend to be happier people because success breeds confidence and confidence makes you feel good about yourself. You know what you are capable of.

It is also important to remember that you may find people who do not have a work ethic, people who do not want to work hard for their dreams. These people may spend their days watching TV or gaming or posting pictures and silly memes on social media.

These are people you need to look out for because they may try to discourage you. They may say that you're wasting your time, that you shouldn't work so hard. *Do not listen to them.* Great things happen when you *set clear goals* for yourself and you *work hard* to *make them happen.*

I'll say this again. Surround yourself with people that support you in the goals that make you a better person. To a great degree *we make our own luck, good or bad, with the choices that we make.* As Seneca said, if you have preparation you will be ready when opportunity comes knocking on your door. If you do not prepare, nothing good will ever really happen. Opportunities will come and go and you will remain stuck in your limitations. The harder and smarter you work the greater your luck.

About Solving Problems, Most Problems:

"Problems are meant to be solved but unfortunately, a lot of people chose to complain, worry and cry about them."

Edmond Mbiaka

"A problem well put is half solved."

John Dewey

"If I had an hour to solve a problem I'd spend 55 minutes thinking about the problem and 5 minutes thinking about the solution."

Albert Einstein

My dear Amaia, sad to say but you will sometimes have problems in life. We all have them and so will you. As one rock band once sang "You can't always get what you want." Problems are a fact of life. As your *abuelo* I wish this weren't true but it is. Some of these problems will be trivial, small. Others will not be small. However, there are some rules that seem to apply to almost all problems. (What follows is a *thought experiment* so don't go around the house looking for matches. Ha, ha, ha.)

Imagine you light a match. Look at that little flame on the top of the short wooden stick. White, yellow and even a bit of blue flicker in that little oval of heat and light. Fire is unique. It's not solid, liquid nor even a gas. The flame is slowly burning its way down and if you hold on to the match long enough without doing anything it's going to reach your fingers and then what? OUCH!!!!! That's what. That tiny little flame is going to burn you and it's going to hurt, a lot.

Now for as long as the flame remains on the head of the match and in your hands you have all the power in the world over it. All you need to do is take a deep breath and blow. That's it. You put out the flame with very little effort and no real damage. (Don't even think about doing the next part of the experiment, ha ha.)

Now let's say you're standing in a puddle of gasoline surrounded by dry leaves and papers. What happens if that flame reaches the gasoline? Now it's not so easy to put out the flame is it? In fact, if you try to blow it now, you may make the fire bigger because the air will actually feed the flame, making it stronger.

Now the trick with most problems in life is to *solve them while they're still small.* Do not procrastinate. If you pretend they are not there most problems will just grow and grow and by the time you finally get around to deal with them they are raging out of control. Then they are much harder to solve.

If you decide to not deal with a problem, *you will in fact be giving up your control over it*. So rule number one is NEVER IGNORE PROBLEMS. Never wait more than you need to. Once you see them set out to fix them as soon as possible. *If you need help, ask for it.* You may need good advice to deal with the challenge.

Rule number two. DEFINE THE PROBLEM AS CLEARLY AND SPECIFICALLY AS YOU POSSIBLY CAN. This means that you must open your eyes, open your ears and shut your mouth. If you cannot see in detail what your challenge is, you will not be able to solve it. That is what both Dewey and Einstein are talking about in the two quotes you read above.

For example, if the problem is with another person try to understand why that person is acting the way she is. In a word, have EMPATHY. When someone speaks to you listen actively to him. *Listen to understand not to respond.* Try to put yourself in the place of the other person. This does not mean that you must agree with the person. It simply means that you try to understand them. Maybe he really is just being a selfish fool that is trying to take advantage of you or… maybe not. Either way, listen and watch people carefully before you decide what you want to do.

When you were a baby your mom was an expert at this. Whenever she heard you crying she would look at you and try to find out why you were so upset. Sometimes it was that you were sleepy or hungry. Sometimes you needed your diaper changed and sometimes, not too often, you were just being a little drama queen that wanted some attention. This applies to things and problems too.

One way of finding out if you truly understand something is by explaining it to someone else. *If you cannot explain a problem simply you simply don't understand it.* If this happens go back and study it some more. Often all it takes is to think intensely about the situation and give yourself some time. Put it in the back of your head and let your mind work with it for a while as you do other things. When you least expect it, the solution will seemingly come out of 'nowhere' and you'll see it.

Some people call it the *sub-conscious* mind. It seems that most people have the ability of thinking about things without being fully aware that they are in fact thinking. Your mind is working on things while you are busy doing other stuff. Even when you sleep your sub-conscious mind is thinking about stuff and looking for solutions or answers. Remember, if needed don't be afraid to ask for help from someone you trust.

Rule number three will probably sound crazy to you but hear me out. Rule number three is ONCE YOU'VE SEEN AND DEFINED THE PROBLEM IGNORE IT. Yes, you heard me. Don't think *about the problem* anymore. Now you need to focus *all* your attention on the SOLUTION to the problem. The dominant question should be "How do we fix this?" If you do that soon enough you will be much more successful than those people who waste their time complaining and whining about problems and challenges. In the case of the flame on the head of your match the solution is simple. Take a deep breath and blow it out.

Notice also that I said how do *we* fix this. No matter how smart you may be you are not Wonder Woman. It is not your job to solve everybody else's problems. Sometimes you have to step back and let others deal with their own things because if you do everything for them they become both dependent and helpless. That is unfair to you and to them. You need to decide if it's *your* problem, *our* problem or *their* problem before moving on.

Now remember that there are different kinds of solutions. Most of the time solutions are *partial*. This means that they may not solve the problem completely. That is fine. As a very smart women once said *"Do what you can with what you have wherever you are."* Some people do not do anything until they find what they claim is the 'perfect' solution. They wait and wait without realizing that the flame is rapidly moving down towards their fingers and the puddle of gasoline at their feet.

Good solutions are often implemented in parts. *If you insist on solving everything all at once you will end up solving nothing.* You may also end up frustrated and very angry. For instance, let's say your mom got you an old car to go to school. The car is in good shape but it needs some things fixed. Perhaps the car needs new tires, the air conditioner repaired and maybe a nice radio. You do not need to fix all those things at once. You *organize them by priority* and you set a time line. Which of these things is more important? Why?

How much will it cost? Fix the most important, most urgent things, first and take it from there.

Finally, realize my dear Amaia that there are some problems in life that may not have solutions. The ultimate problem for most people is of course the end of life, death. I realized that fully when I was hospitalized shortly after your birth. Death is simply a fact of life. All things must pass including us.

Knowing about my mortality did not make me lose my appreciation for all the wonderful things that life brings, like the chance of meeting new and wonderful people, like you. So one of my solutions was to write these words for you. It may not be a perfect solution but I know it's probably one of the best ones under the circumstances. Even after I'm gone I can still be a small part of your life.

So, when dealing with the problems of life, start working on them as soon as you can. Define them as clearly as you can and look for solutions. When you finally understand them focus on the possible options available to you. Oh, and as I said before, never be afraid to ask for help.

About Failure:

"In order to succeed you must fail, *so that you know what not to do* next time."

Anthony D'Angelo

Dear Amaia don't be afraid of making some mistakes. That is how you will grow and learn about all the stuff that will catch your eyes. You can't learn how to ride a bike without falling over more than once. You can't learn how to swim without jumping into the water and getting your butt wet. The more you practice something, a sport, a musical instrument or a recipe, the more mistakes you make, the more you will learn and the better you will get at it. That's just how life works.

The good thing is that you do not have to go at it alone. You have your family who loves you beyond words and are there to support you. You may also find good people that know how to do what you're interested in learning. You can ask for their help.

Most good people are very happy to help others. These people are called *mentors*. Good mentors can help you grow and become better at what you're learning. Join groups that share your goals and your love for something. Also, once you become good at something, share what you've learned with others. You can then become the one to help somebody else learn and grow and you can in time become their mentor.

A very wise man once said that *there is greater happiness in giving than in receiving.* There is more truth in those words that most people realize. Turns out that *by helping others we often find that we're really helping ourselves.* Roberto Clemente, a Boricua just like you and me, and one of the world's greatest baseball players of all time once said that if you let a day go by without helping others you have wasted that day. That, I think, is very true. Helping others is a way of showing ourselves that we have learned from our mistakes.

As an English professor I sometimes had students that were so afraid of making mistakes that they did not want to speak out loud in a second language. They thought others would laugh at them. Well, it so happens that there is no way anyone can learn a first, second or fourth language without making mistakes. These are *a necessary part* of learning. They even have a name. They're called *developmental* errors. Errors are how we all experiment, try things out, in life.

You learn how to cook by having a few failed meals. You will serve that first meal and your victims, I mean your friends, will taste it, smile and say it's just fine when in reality it was way too salty or perhaps overcooked. But because they don't want to hurt your feelings they may wash the whole thing down with water, juice or a cold beer.

Others may not be so nice when pointing out your mistakes. They may be blunt or maybe even a bit rude. Have patience with these people too and see if their criticism is valid. *If what they say is true* then suck up your pride and make the changes you need to do to fix things.

Warning, if you do something once and you have bad results, THAT is a mistake. If you do that same dumb thing a second or third time *knowing what will happen* that IS NOT a mistake. That is a choice. Do not confuse the two. Many people confuse them and that is why they suffer needlessly. They become their own worst enemies by making bad choices over and over again. It is just plain crazy to expect better results if we insist on doing the same stupid things again and again.

Just one more thing about mistakes. Try to always focus intensely on what you're doing because some mistakes can be very, very costly. If you burn up that rice you were preparing for dinner, no big deal. If you burn down the kitchen or the house, hmm, big deal. Same thing goes with driving. You do not want to make a bad decision while moving at 60 miles an hour on a rainy road with a bunch of people in your car. For instance, if you get very sleepy while driving find a safe place, park and take a nap. Do not make the mistake of driving while sleepy. This is very dangerous indeed.

The laws of physics do not care who you are. If you do something wrong the results will be immediate and the consequences may be terrible. Make your mistakes but always try to limit their size and frequency and always learn from them so that next time they become fewer and less serious.

Failing is a necessary part of eventual success. You can't have one without the other. When you fall down just take a deep breath, get up and try again.

About Discrimination and Pride:

"With pride there are many curses. With humility there are many blessings."

Ezra Taft Benson

"Show *class*, have *pride* and display *character*. If you do, winning will take care of itself."

Paul Bryant

I decided to discuss discrimination and pride together because they have one thing in common. They can be either incredibly bad or amazingly good. Let's look at the bad side first. Sadly, there is a lot of bad discrimination going on around in the world. Discrimination is sometimes described with words that end with 'ism'. Things like rac*ism* and sex*ism* are two good examples of bad discrimination. As you grow older you may realize that some men may think that you are somehow not as good as they are because you are a female, a girl. They may think that you are not as smart as boys are or that you should not to be treated the same way a boy or a man is treated.

This type of discrimination is very bad because it denies you the same opportunities, rights and protection that are given to males. There are many crazy ideas that develop around this gender discrimination. For example, women drivers are generally believed to be terrible drivers. There are all kinds of jokes about how bad women drive. The truth may be precisely the opposite.

Automobile insurance companies study the likelihood of different kinds of drivers having serious accidents so they can decide how much to charge for their services. You pay these companies money, usually a monthly a fee, and they will pay you money so you can fix your car if you have an accident. So insurance companies need to know how much of a risk you are as a driver.

It turns out that the most dangerous drivers on the road are young males. Year after year they have more serious car accidents than any other group of drivers evaluated. That's why they must pay more money for the same insurance protection than women. You don't have to take my word for this. When you get your first driver's license visit an insurance company with a male friend of your same age and ask about the cost of car insurance. See how much it will cost you and him. He's going to be very surprised.

Racism is also a very, very bad form of discrimination. This is the idea that you can tell if a person is good or bad, smart or dumb, depending on their race or ethnicity. Although we may look different on the outside all people are the same on the inside. Native Americans, blacks, Asians, Hispanics, most of which are brown people, have all been victims of terrible discrimination at different moments of American history.

Others have also been discriminated because of their religious beliefs. The Irish and the Italians who moved to the US in the early XX century were rejected by many because they were Catholics. However, *if religious beliefs do not constitute a threat* to the well-being and freedom of others this discrimination is also wrong. There are good people in almost all faiths.

These two types of discrimination, sexism and racism, are often based on lies, ignorance and fear. People tend to fear what they do not understand. When they see others who speak differently, dress differently, have a different culture they often reject them. If they're not careful that fear can very easily become hate, thus prejudice is born.

Truth of the matter is that *we are all one species*, one people, one race, the *human* race. This is not an opinion. It's a fact. Science has shown that we are all homo-sapiens-sapiens. That's our scientific name. We are all but one species.

Yet discrimination need not be a bad thing. Some kinds of discrimination are not only acceptable, they are essential for you to make good decisions in life. Let's say you are shopping for a new pair of shoes. Do you just buy the first pair you see at the very first store? Hmm... I don't think so. Most people will look around. They will compare styles, price, fit and quality. They will try on a few pairs and then decide which one to buy. When you do this you are discriminating. You are comparing shoes and then you are judging them. You are deciding which pair is best for you in terms of your specific needs and wants.

This kind of discrimination is smart and very much needed for a happy life. If you do not take the time to practice this kind of discrimination *in all aspects of your life* you may end up with things or people you don't really need around you.

Now let's take a look at the other term, pride. There are two basic kinds of pride. The first one is very bad if not watched over carefully. This is the feeling of success we get from *other* people's accomplishments. For instance, when you are watching a sporting event, a basketball or a soccer game you may be rooting for a specific team. You want your team to win. If that team wins then you may jump up and down screaming "*We* won! *We* won!"

But if you think about it for a moment you'll realize that *you didn't really win* at all. You did not practice your sport with the other teammates for years on end. You did not run five miles every morning to get in shape. Yet you feel like you won because that's the Orlando Magic or the Miami Heat. That team represents you and millions of other fans.

Now there is nothing wrong with watching sports and celebrating your team's success just as long as that kind of pride does not become your *main source of feelings of accomplishment*. This kind of pride is a lazy thing. You take part in the celebration of somebody else's hard work and success.

The good kind of pride is different. It is that great feeling you get after YOU have done something important for yourself or others. For example, say you have a big biology test coming up and your friends invite you to the beach. You want to go with them but you need to stay home and study. There we go, a clash between what you want and what you need. What would you do? Ha, ha. I can almost hear you saying the beach. Well, I hope that's not always the case. Now let's say you have strong will power and you stay home and study for the test. The next morning you take the exam and you ace it. You get a 94, a good solid A. You feel good, you feel proud.

That is the pride you should always have within you, *the satisfaction of a job well done.* People who understand the difference between these two prides are unstoppable. They know how important it is to work hard to make things, good things, happen. They know how important it is to ALWAYS do the very best that they can and finish what they start.

So if you discriminate intelligently for valid reasons and you take pride in your own accomplishments you too will reach your goals in life. Your dreams will come true because you made them come true.

About Health and Eating:

"Let food by thy medicine."

Hipporates

"All you need is love. But a little chocolate now and then doesn't hurt you."

Charles M. Schulz, creator of Charlie Brown and Peanuts

Eat less and better and move more. That's all you really need to do. I hope the world you live in has as much food as mine did. It is good to have so many choices in the form of fruits, vegetables, cheeses, grains and so many other kinds of food. However, having many choices can sometimes be very bad.

For many people of my time this abundance of food options creates a big, big problem. Many people of my generation have *too much* food and seven out of every ten are overweight. We don't move around much either. There are many reasons for this. First, it's our addiction to TV, which initially became popular back in 1953. We spend way too much time watching television.

When I was growing up in the 1960's in New York City most people had only three TV channels, NBC, CBS and ABC. That was it. At first, everything was in black and white. Can you believe that? No color television. No control over the scheduling either. You couldn't record anything or watch a show or a movie at your convenience. If you missed it, that was it. Rarely did you get a second chance any time soon. You had to wait for the reruns to come and watch them the second time around if you were lucky.

Thanks to TV old movies got a second chance to reach the people. When TVs became popular there was nearly 50 years' worth of old movies that found new life on the small home screens. Great old movies like *It's a Wonderful Life* which was originally in theaters in 1943 were rediscovered by millions of TV viewers ten years later.

The Wizard of Oz with Judy Garland, a great movie from the 1930s, also found new life when homes got their first TV sets in the 1950s. It even became a Christmas tradition to watch them once a year with family and friends.

Then came the great sitcoms, *I love Lucy, The Jackie Gleason Show* and finally my personal favorite *The Twilight Zone,* a weird fantasy show hosted by Rod Serling that explored strange topics and rarely had a happy ending.

By the mid-1960s the first color TVs started to make their way into homes all over America and Puerto Rico. With them came full color programs like *the Flintstones, Batman, Looney Tunes* and *Tom and Jerry.*

Then some years later we got cable TV. Now we had dozens of TV shows and channels and we had what they called syndicated shows. These were old TV shows that were aired all over again for a new audience. After cable came satellite TV and by the time you were born everybody and their grandmother had High Definition, HD, sets that were just unbelievably clear and detailed.

Tablets and smart phones even allowed people to take their TV shows with them wherever they went. With platforms like *Netflix* or *Amazon Prime* now you decided when and what to watch.

All this was lovely to look at but not very good for our health. Too many people forgot that their *bodies were made for walking, running and climbing.* They got slow, and lazy and overweight and even sick. Some doctors even compared this sedentary life style to a nasty habit called smoking. Tobacco smoking is a very dangerous habit that has hurt and killed millions of people. Well, someone said that *sitting was the new smoking.*

Not using your body the way nature intended is just as bad for you as smoking tobacco.

Sad but true. They even made an animated movie called *Wall E* that showed a future world where nature and health were killed by a human society that consumed way too much but exercised very, very little.

The world of *Wall E* was a world in which humanity abused nature and killed the planet, a society that forgot that *we didn't inherit our planet from our parents. We borrowed it from you, our children.* The people in Wall E were compulsive on-line consumers that did little or no exercise and humanity was thus *voluntarily* bedridden. Sad.

So what is your *abuelo* trying to tell you? Simple. Don't become lazy and waste your time sitting in front of a screen all day long. It doesn't matter if it's a computer screen, a tablet, a smart phone or an HD-TV. Enjoy these things *in moderation.* Keep on doing exercise and shake that bootie. If you like, do sports, jump and run around.

Food is the other important health issue. After much research, science found out a lot of great things about how to care for your body and health. *Eat less and eat better.* Over-eating can be just as bad as not eating enough. In many developed countries people just love to eat meats, pork, beef, chicken and other animals. Turns out that *eating meat is not good for us.* Meats, especially red meats, cause all sorts of diseases like cancer, diabetes, arteriosclerosis and high blood pressure.

Scientists found that they are very bad for our health. In fact, that may be the main reason why I got my heart attack. My Puerto Rican diet was just full of red meats. *pernil*, pork chops, steaks and the like were all a daily part of my breakfast, lunch and dinner. Very tasty but not very healthy.

Junk food is another clear danger. This is food that is very tasty but not very nutritional. It is high in calories, fat, sugar and sometimes even toxic chemicals. All these things are very bad for your body. When you were born this kind of food was everywhere. Fast food restaurants would get you a cheap and tasty meal for a few dollars yet the quality of this food was awful.

Check out the documentary *Supersize Me* for details. Your mom was always very careful not to feed you this bad food. As you grow older *you must learn to do this on your own.*

If you want to remain healthy *make sure your food is mostly plant based.* Eat vegetables, fresh fruits, beans, some whole grain breads or brown rice. Eat for pleasure but also eat to get the energy you need to live your life to the fullest. A documentary titled *Fork over Knives* can give you some great ideas as to how to control your diet and thus protect your health. Look it up. If you *eat less and you move more* you will enjoy a longer and healthier life. It's that simple.

You will learn in time to use different things to prepare meals. Some things can make your food better by allowing you to prepare your meals in a safe, tasty way. Others may not be so good. Stay away from *aluminum cookware*. Aluminum pots and pans have toxins that can leak bad chemicals into your food. These can make you very sick. Use instead *food grade* stainless steel pots and pans. These will not poison your food. Also bake and prepare food in glass containers, never in aluminum pots or foil.

Also stay away from something called Teflon. This is a non-stick coating that is used on many pots and pans so the food doesn't stick to the pans. It too has very dangerous chemicals that can leak into your food and make you very sick.

Oh, one more thing. Get enough sleep. Sleep is how we recharge our bodies for the next day. Not sleeping enough can be very harmful to you. You can research this on your own so look it up when you can. Educate yourself on how to best feed yourself, how to exercise and how to rest. *Those who love you are very much aware of this so I'm sure they will help you develop the right habits. Listen to them.*

About Freedom:

"Responsibility is the price of freedom."

Elbert Hubbard

"A hero is someone who understands the responsibility that comes with his freedom."

Bob Dylan

"Just because you *can* do something it *doesn't mean you should* do it."

Anonymous

Freedom is a very popular word. Almost everybody speaks about it, about how we all need to be free. Many people think that freedom is to be able to do whatever you want, whenever you want and wherever you want. All that may be true *to a point* but it is a bit more complicated than that. Let me explain.

Freedom is more than just being able to do whatever we want. Freedom is a form of power and power in the wrong hands can be a very dangerous thing. For example, a chainsaw is a powerful tool. When cutting wood it can slice thru thick branches with ease. You can use the wood to feed a campfire, cook a meal and keep warm. You can even build a house with the wood that has been cut with a powerful saw.

Yet if not used properly it can slice thru an arm or a leg with equal ease and terrible consequences. So its power must be controlled. In fact, *power without control is not only useless, it can be very dangerous.* This is true about chainsaws and just about everything else in life.

So, people must learn that as Spiderman's late uncle once said *"With great power comes great responsibility"*. Just because that was said by a comic book character it doesn't mean it's not true. It is very true. Your mom, for example, may limit your freedom at first and expect you to earn more and more freedom *as you show her that you are mature, trustworthy and honest* enough to handle it.

As you *earn her trust* she will allow you to do more and more things on your own. If you do not earn her trust she will not grant you more power, more freedom. Now, how exactly can you earn that trust? That's simple. *Keep your word.* If you say you're going to do something, do it. Do it completely. Do it the best you can. Do it when you said you would. *Do it even if nobody is looking.* Show mom that she can believe in you.

This also applies in school and work settings. At a job you may be asked to do things that at first may seem unimportant, trivial. You may think they're dumb or way too easy for you. Do them anyway and do them well. As you prove that you can be counted on, you will be trusted with more important things.

However, if you mess up with the so-called 'little' things you may not be trusted with bigger responsibilities. In other words, *for freedom to be a good thing for you it must be earned by you.* You must show yourself and others that you are capable of handling responsibilities productively and safely.

If you give an irresponsible person the freedom of having and driving a car, for example, you may be giving him the instrument of his own destruction. Just recently, early 2017, I read the sad story of a young man, maybe twenty years old, who had a terrible car accident in San Sebastian, your grandparent's home town. The young man was racing a car his parents had given him to drive to and from school. He lost control and had a terrible accident. He was given freedom and he abused it. He died on a road near his home. As you can imagine his family was heartbroken. They did not realize that he was not yet ready for having a car.

Another example of dangerous freedom can be found in the way we use the Internet. For instance, when we go on line we have the freedom to go anywhere we want. Behind closed doors we may feel that no one is watching and we may feel tempted to go to dangerous websites, dangerous places. Well, freedom should not be the notion that anything goes. Remember, JUST BECAUSE YOU CAN DO SOMETHING IT DOESN'T MEAN YOU SHOULD.

Most people do not eat garbage. We don't drink motor oil or other toxic stuff. We know it would hurt us. Well, *if we don't put trash in our mouth why would we put trash in our minds?* So-called *entertainment* that encourages harmful conduct should be avoided. There are websites that encourage hate, prejudice, violence and sexism. There are people who promote divisions and racism. *Some criminals even surf the net looking for victims.* They may pretend to be your age and join a chat group to gain your trust and come into your life.

These people use the Internet to do harm. Don't waste one minute listening or watching them. Do not use your freedom to feed your heart and mind with these terrible things. You wouldn't allow a bad person to come into your home. So why would you allow them to come into your mind and heart thru the Internet? Bad ideas can destroy anyone just as surely as poison or guns can. Do not abuse your freedom.

There are different kinds of freedom. We have freedom of speech, freedom to gather in groups and the freedom to travel. Economic freedom, of course, is also very important.

In 2016, your year, there were many people arguing about these freedoms. Some people thought that we had too much of these freedoms and others were convinced that we did not have enough of them. Who was right? How could we know?

I am not going to go deep into the philosophical implications of these questions. As you grow older you may want to explore them in detail on your own. I will briefly discuss these issues from what I feel is a purely practical point of view.

The freedom to speak, for instance, is extremely important. In any and all relationships you should feel comfortable enough to express your true feelings and speak your mind. If someone does not respect you enough to recognize that fundamental right you have, to honestly speak your mind, just walk away and do so quickly.

However remember that the right to speak can never include the right to abuse or bully anybody. Someone once said, "Sticks and stones can break my bones but words can never hurt me." That is not true. Words can hurt people…. a lot. They can destroy a person's self-esteem, make them feel that they are worthless. Never do this to anyone and of course do not allow anyone to do this to you. There is a Chinese proverb that suggests that before speaking we should always ask ourselves three questions:

- Is it true?
- Is it kind?

- Will it help?

Truthfulness when we speak is very important. For starters, when you say the truth you do not have to keep track of everything you said because you were honest. Liars on the other hand need to have very good memories because all it takes is one truth to bring down a mountain of lies.

Truthfulness also builds trust, the basis for all good relationships. When a person is known for keeping her word and respectfully speaking her mind other honest people are attracted to her.

Kindness is another important aspect when using your freedom of speech. Words can help heal a broken heart or they can destroy a life. There is a lovely Native American story that has an elderly man speaking with his grandchild. The grandfather warns the younger one that inside every person there are two wolves in constant battle.

One wolf represents anger, hate, greed and all the bad things that can destroy him. The other wolf represents truthfulness, mercy, empathy, love and all the good things that can make a person stronger, better. The boy looked up at his grandfather and asked, "Which wolf wins?"

The old man answered, "The one you feed." That is a choice that we all must make on a daily basis. Are we going to use our freedom to feed the good wolf or the bad one? Some people feed the bad one by being verbally abusive to others and ignoring their needs and emotions. I hope you always do your best to feed the good wolf in you. But don't you forget that the bad wolf will always be there too.

The third question, "Will it help?" is also a very wise thing to ask. When others are struggling to solve a problem they may need support. Sometimes words can encourage them to try harder and make progress. Sometimes words can take away the will to fight and go on. What effect will *your* words have?

Always think about these three things BEFORE you speak because once words are spoken they cannot be taken back. No matter how sorry you may feel.

The freedom of assembly, the right to be part of any group you want to be a part of, is also fundamental. However, you should be very careful about which groups you decide to join. There are many very good groups out there. At my university, the University of Puerto Rico, many students form groups that allow them to work with other people that have similar interests. There are chemistry, biology, education and ESL student organizations. Gathering with others that share the same interests and goals that you have can be a very good idea. Groups give us a sense of belonging and support.

But not all groups are good. If you hang out with the wrong people you may find yourself in a lot of trouble. You see, there's this thing called the Lucifer Effect. Social scientists have found that people have the tendency to follow very closely the behaviors of whatever groups they belong to. If the group starts doing things that are violent, irresponsible or even dangerous to themselves or others many people will just go along.

The individual then is no longer free. She has now become a slave to the group she has joined. (For details, research the Stanford Prison Experiment by Philip Zimbardo or watch his TED talk.)

The same thing applies to the freedom to travel. You were born into a world in which travelling is a fairly easy thing. You can save some money, buy a ticket and travel all over the place. Within a city you can also go almost anywhere you like. Yet again, just because you can do something it doesn't mean you should. There are places that are torn by crime, violence and other serious social problems. Before you decide to go anywhere find out how safe it is for you and those who travel with you.

For instance, before visiting an unfamiliar city or country do a bit of research and if possible find someone who knows the place you want to visit well. When it comes to traveling, our ignorance will not protect us. If we go to the wrong place at the wrong time we will get into trouble.

Finally, we get to economic freedom. Here I am going to quote one of America's greatest presidents, Franklyn Delano Roosevelt. He once said, "True individual *freedom cannot exist without economic security* and independence. People who are hungry and out of a job are the stuff of which dictatorships are made."

As you grow older and wiser you will slowly take more and more control of your life. It will start with little things like what to wear of what movie to see. In time, this will include your choices regarding how you decide to help yourself and others. You may ask yourself big questions like,

"What do I want to do with my life? What should I study?"

You will need a job to take care of yourself and your loved ones. I became a college professor. I was very lucky because it turned out to be a very good choice for me. I get paid for helping others learn English and thus make their lives better. I am not rich but I make enough money to care of myself and those I love. This career gave me the freedom to support and help others in many good ways.

Making a living, earning enough money, will give you more options. This power of choice is an important form of freedom. Most jobs involve trading a given amount of time for a given amount of money. Now remember, *time is life itself.*

If we end up giving too much time for too little money we won't really have much freedom at all. We may live from check to check and week to week just to pay the bills that seem to never end.

That's why having a good education is so important. The more skilled you are the more likely it is that you will get a job that'll let you protect more of your time, thus your personal freedom.

If you can make a living by doing something you really enjoy you're going to be a very happy person. *Turning your vacation into your vocation is a wonderful thing*. People that are stuck in a job that is not meaningful to them are rarely very happy. On the other hand, those who love what they do don't really feel like they're working at all.

Some years ago two very famous singers, Willy Nelson and Paul Mc Cartney, were speaking about retirement. Paul asked Willy what did he think about retirement. Willy Nelson, a super famous country artist, seemed puzzled. "Retire from what?" he asked. Willy Nelson loved his job as an artist so much he didn't even think of it as work so he saw no need to retire. In his opinion he wasn't working at all. Ha ha...

However, this is not to say that you shouldn't have, at least when you're younger, a job you hate. Unfortunately sometimes that's all there is. Take Chris, one of my graduating students in 2016. He was one of my best students and almost every week I would see him at a local supermarket. He had a part-time job there. He did everything in that place, take out the trash, collect shopping carts from the parking lot and stock the shelves. It turns out Chris hated working there. He was overworked, underpaid and miserable. Balancing his classes and the job was very difficult sometimes.

Yet he stayed there because he needed the money. He had to pay for his dorm, his food and keep his car going. His family helped but it wasn't enough. Chris stayed there for nearly three years because *he knew it was only temporary*. With the right education Chris knew that he would find a much better job in the future.

You may find that you do not want to work for others. Maybe you will build your own business and support yourself and others in that way. That is something that you will in time discover. No need to rush. Look inside your heart and find out what it is that you enjoy doing that makes you feel good and at the same time helps others. Find out what you are really good at and focus on that.

Once you know why you're here, dedicate yourself heart and soul to it. You will find that taking care of yourself will be so much easier when you have a feeling of accomplishment and service to others. Being independent, having the freedom to do what you want to do career-wise is a wonderful thing. You will need to have a good education to achieve this so *stay in school, set your goals* and *make good things happen*.

The worse kind of slavery is *mental* slavery, ignorance and prejudice. Bob Marley, a popular singer, once said something that I believe is very true, "Emancipate yourself from mental slavery none but yourself can free your mind." Feed your mind and heart with good ideas and good experiences. Read good books, grow and learn and do as much as you can. When you use your freedom wisely all other good things will follow. Always feed the good wolf. That's what your *abuelo* thinks.

About Love:

"Love all, trust a few, do wrong to none."

William Shakespeare

"I don't trust people who don't love themselves and tell me, 'I love you.' ... There is an African saying which is: "Be careful when a naked man offers you a shirt.""

Maya Angelou

I guess that you know by now that you are loved by many people. You came to our family at a time when no one was really expecting you. Everybody was so excited to know that you were on your way. You were our first grandchild on both sides of the family. We didn't know you yet but we were all anxious to meet you.

Love is a special thing that is present in many kinds of relationships. Some people even divide it into different kinds of love. A very long time ago the ancient Greeks, for example, had specific words for different kinds of love. They spoke about the love of friends and family, the love of romance and other kinds of love. *Love connects us to someone or something.* It includes feelings but it must also have actions. When we love we care. Our love becomes obvious in the way we treat each other.

But before going on perhaps it's a good idea to clearly state *what love is not,* what it never does. Love never, ever harms the object of its affection. NEVER. Love is not possessive or restrictive. It cannot be forced nor imposed. If someone uses love as an excuse to try to control you beware because *that* is not love. *A person who truly loves you will never try to hurt you.*

Also, distrust is never a part of true love. If a person is jealous and seeks to control you, that person does not deserve your love. If you have good reason to distrust a person because of the way he acts then move away. Your affection should not be wasted on someone who does not deserve it. Love does not tie people down or make them feel afraid or insecure.

If someone ever tries to do this to you *stop it immediately*. If needed, get help from others but <u>do not stay in a relationship that makes you feel bad and can harm you.</u> That obsessive conduct may go by many other names but it is not love.

Also be very careful with what or who you love. When you were born many of the young adults that made up your parents' generation, the millennials, were gamers. They *loved* sitting in front of their Play Stations or X Boxes and play these great video-games for hours on end. Great colors and sounds and amazing plots and special effects made for a lot of fun and good entertainment. It was like getting into a movie and becoming the main character. However there was a down side to all this fun.

As I said earlier many did not exercise much. They were sedentary. They spent way too much time sitting still. It wasn't only that many were physically sedentary. They were also mentally and emotionally sedentary. Technology allowed them to carry their games with them in many devices including their cell phones. Someone once called these people smart-phone zombies.

You would go to a restaurant and you would see a family of four sitting at a table and no one was looking at each other or talking. Everybody was focused on their own device. They were sitting together but they weren't really together. This is an easy way to destroy relationships. If you truly care and love someone *put the damn phone away and have a real conversation.* Look and listen to the person attentively. Expect that the other person do the same when they speak to you.

Nature has a very simple rule that applies to everyone. *You use it or loss it. So falling in love with gaming or social media to the point where you do not connect with other people sitting right beside you is a very bad thing.* Your mom knows this so hopefully you will grow up knowing the value of good exercise and paying attention to people in a healthy, happy life.

Falling in love with people or habits that hurt us is very dangerous. When it comes to people, *never beg for anyone's attention or love.* Remember, no one can ever force anyone else to love them. That's not how it works. So always respect and *love yourself* enough to know that you deserve better.

If someone is incapable of giving you the time, respect and attention that you need and deserve then that person does not belong with you. *Just move on* and continue with your own life. It may hurt at first but it will be for the good of you and the others too.

Never forget to *love yourself first*. Respect yourself and know that you should never have low expectations. *Those who expect and accept little from life will get just that, little from life.* Very often life will only give you what you believe you deserve. If you do not love yourself first you cannot really love others. *One cannot give what one does not have.* If you do not respect yourself it will be difficult for others to respect you.

Loving yourself means always taking care of yourself. Eat right, do exercise, rest well. Your body is not a trash can so don't put garbage in it. Some people abuse substances that slowly kill them. Addiction to food, alcohol or drugs are common problems for many people. Your body will give you warning signs when you neglect or abuse it.

If you drink too much alcohol you will likely get something called a hangover. Headaches, throwing up, feeling dizzy are common symptoms. This is your body telling you that you disrespected it. It's asking you to pay attention and not do that again. *Pain* then *becomes a good thing*. It is a warning system that helps you make positive changes in your habits. You love yourself when you listen to these warnings. So *loving yourself means taking care of yourself*. Only then will you be ready to love others successfully.

Once you have a loving relationship with someone take care of it. This applies even to your family. Love, like a house plant, needs to be cared for and protected. If a relationship is neglected it will slowly but surely die. Good deeds, honesty, attentiveness all make love grow. Listening with empathy and understanding make love grow. Saying little things like thank you, may I help you, or asking if someone is OK can go a long way in keeping people connected to each other. That is a key element for happiness. *We all need to be connected to other people, friends and family, to feel safe, healthy and strong.* We humans are social creatures.

Dishonesty, negligence and indifference will kill any relationship. Someone once said that human relationships are a bit like bank accounts. You need to make deposits in order to make withdrawals. Healthy relationships need a steady flow of give and take. Whenever someone just takes and takes from a relationship they will end up emptying the 'account'. Not a good thing.

Be aware of people that are only takers. If ignored they can do a lot of harm to you. They can drain your emotions, waste your time and your money. The opposite is also true. If one person constantly gives and gives and never gets anything in return she will grow tired and bored.

Do not allow others to take advantage of you. If someone brings nothing of value to your life because of their bad and selfish attitudes *let them go*. You will run into people that will only remember you whenever they are in trouble or when they need something. That is not love and they are not real friends. They are simply manipulators that are motivated by greedy self-interest. Trust only those that have thru their actions shown you that they deserve your friendship and love.

About Money:

"Money without brains is always a dangerous thing."

Napoleon Hill

"Never spend your money before you have earned it."

Thomas Jefferson

"A fool and her money soon go separate ways."

Anonymous

"For *the love* of money is the root of all kinds of evils."

Apostle Paul

Money is good. Money is needed and money can give you something wonderful. If used properly, it can give you *freedom* and *peace of mind*. In our Western society it is a very important thing. For example, if you need food or a place to stay or maybe transportation, money will allow you to get these things even in a country or city that is new to you and where you have no friends or family.

Money is a medium of exchange that allows you to trade these rectangular pieces of paper or small metal discs for *things of real value* like food, clothing, transportation or medical attention. Money allows you to carry a small plastic card that will give you real options in times of need. It is very good to have and use.

However, always remember this. *Money is a wonderful slave but a terrible master*. It is simply a very useful tool. Nothing more.

Sadly, money has become a kind of god for many. They feel that if only they had a lot of money life would be perfect. Unfortunately that is not true. Greed is bad, very bad. It makes people do terrible things to get money. Some people lie, steal and even hurt others so they can have the money they are convinced will finally bring them happiness. A very famous early Christian called the Apostle Paul expressed it very nicely, "For *the love of money* is the root of all kinds of evils." Money is to be used not worshiped. Notice that Paul doesn't say that money is bad. He explains that *the love of money* is the root of all evil.

No. Having a lot of money will not bring you happiness. Once your basic needs are covered, a safe place to live, good food, a good education and adequate medical care, a lot more money will not do much to enhance your life and sense of well-being.

Money has no special powers to really change people for the better. If I am a poor fool and I suddenly hit the lottery I simply become a rich fool. What's more, fools with a lot of money tend to get into more trouble than penniless fools because their new found wealth makes their power to get into big trouble that much greater. Scientist Carl Sagan once observed that power plus ignorance equaled trouble. That is what money is, power, and if used incorrectly it can cause a lot of pain.

Science has found that money sometimes brings out the worse in people. A TED talk I saw once spoke about this issue. It was called 'Does money make you mean?' by Paul Piff. The talk described a series of experiments in which people were made to feel that they were rich by using a board game called Monopoly. The way they behaved and treated others was then analyzed. Scientists found that many people did in fact become mean and arrogant with unjustified feelings of superiority. They really thought they were somehow better than those who had less wealth.

When people become obsessed with accumulating large amounts of money they often forget about family and friends. They may neglect their need to sleep, eat healthy, exercise or share with loved ones. All they often do is work, work and work. There's even a word for them, *workaholics.* They may end up doing the most foolish exchange of all, trading large amounts of time for money. That is a very bad deal because *time, not money, is by far our most important resource.*

When people combine their *uncontrolled love for money* with the devil of *valueless consumerism* they get into BIG trouble. They want to buy, buy and buy but since they don't have enough money to get the things they want they do something very foolish. They go into large amounts of *debt.* Whole cities and nations have fallen into this trap and they have paid for it with blood, pain and tears.

When this thing called debt comes into the picture terrible things can happen. Some people get others to give them something called *credit.* Now they can buy what they want with other people's money with the promise to pay it back with something called *interests*. This means that if you give me $100 dollars so I can buy something I will pay you back $120 dollars within a specific amount of weeks or months. Those $20 extra dollars are the penalty, the interest, I have to pay for having used your money for my wants.

Store owners, banks and sales people all want you to spend as much money as possible on their stuff so *they will make it very easy for you to get credit*. They may offer you credit cards or credit lines so that you can buy whatever it is that they are selling. Do not fall for it Amaia.

Debt can become a chain that will turn you into a slave just as effectively as actual chains hold back people under traditional slavery. If you choose not to pay back the money you got from a lender they will damage your credit rating. They will tell others that you are not reliable, that you do not keep your promises. Thus others will not give you any additional credit.

This can be very bad because it means that if you need to buy something expensive like a house or a car no one will give you credit. For these 'big ticket' items you need to have a good credit rating. Lenders need to know that you keep your promises.

Now, this is not to say that you shouldn't have debt. As I said above, in life you may need to buy some things on credit. For example, a car or house are usually too expensive to pay all at once so you may pay some of it with something called a *down payment* and then pay the rest of it with monthly payments for a number of years. Nothing wrong with that.

However, always keep your debt down to a small fraction of what your total monthly *income* is. Income is the money you make with your job, whatever this may be. Also, when working, always pay yourself first. Instead of always thinking about how much you're going to *spend*, focus on how much you're going to *save*. Try not to spend money you don't have by abusing your credit and getting into unneeded debt.

Spend most of your money on *things you truly need not things you simply want*. Always know the difference between these two. Needs are *things we must have to live* and wants are *things that* may be nice but *are not essential.* You need good food to keep yourself healthy. You do not need to buy it in an expensive restaurant. You need nice, comfortable and durable clothing. You do not need them to be of a special, expensive name brand. Do not allow flashy commercials to lure you into the trap of mindless consumption. Do not worry about impressing others with the things you have.

Remember that your *real friends* love you *for who you are not what you have*. What acquaintances or strangers think about you shouldn't be so important. So don't worry too much about impressing them. A French philosopher once said that *some people spend money they don't have on things they don't need to impress people they don't even like*. Ha, ha, that is so true. Don't be one of them. Always use your brain before using your money. Remember a fool and her money soon go separate ways. Never be a consumeristic fool. It's better to have $280 in a $20 purse than to have an empty $300 purse.

About Religion:

"My religion is very simple. My religion is kindness."

Dalai Lama

"When I do good I feel good. When I do bad I feel bad. That is my religion."

Abraham Lincoln

This is a topic I feel a bit uncomfortable with because it causes a lot of arguments and sometimes people get very angry defending or attacking different points of view. But it is such an important subject that I cannot ignore it.

Personally, I am an *agnostic* but I will try to be as fair as I can here without misrepresenting the opinion of others. An agnostic is a person who is in the middle of believers and non-believers. One who denies the existence of a god is usually called an *atheist*. A believer in God is called a *theist*. Well, I am not sure who to believe. I do not think I have enough good reasons to believe either group so I stay neutral.

I am sure you are smart enough and as you grow older you will look around and hear what different people say about religion and faith and the supernatural. So listen to what they say and make your own choices. Ask a lot of questions. Just remember my dear child, when exploring religion please *use your mind as much as you use your heart.*

I will start off by saying that some religions seem to promote good ideas and values while others seem to promote ignorance and fear. When those who call themselves Christians really believe in Christ's central message they can bring people together and promote peace and understanding. There are many good people in *almost* all religions and faiths.

When you were born there was a very good Christian man called Jimmy Carter. He was an American president and when he retired from politics he spent most of his life helping many poor families get their own homes by working with a group called Habitat for Humanity. For many years he used his time, his fame as a former president and all his influence to bring thousands of volunteers together to help others build their own homes. I admired Carter very much. He and others like him were true promoters of much needed good in a world that is often divided by hate, violence and distrust.

However, there are religions that are not good. I will not go into specifics here but I will warn you of some things you need to be careful with. Any religion that *tries to separate* you from your family, friends and loved ones is a bad religion. *Isolation is needed for manipulation.* Some will try to scare you by saying that if you read this or listen to that you will offend God. Their true goal is censorship. They want to control you by controlling what you read or watch. They may tell you that you should only listen to them because only they have the truth. Do not allow anyone to do that to you. No one has a monopoly of truth.

For example, any religion that promotes the idea that *women are somehow less capable*, or in any way *inferior to men* is a bad religion. In some churches God and Scripture, whatever holy book they believe in, are often used as excuses to give men power over women. That should be completely unacceptable to you or any other self-respecting person, male or female.

Also any religion that *rejects reason and science* and instead depends on songs, emotions and noisy cults is a bad religion. If a faith cannot convince you with respect, evidence and reasonable arguments it is not to be trusted. Feelings, no matter how intense, are no substitute of facts or reason.

Finally, any religion that *is afraid of answering your questions* and *tries to silence* you is a very bad religion. If its members say that you will go to hell if you do not do as they tell you they are not a good people. A loving, heavenly father would never torture his children to control then, even if they did not obey him.

A very smart man I have quoted here a few times, Albert Einstein, wrote a very interesting essay on the subject called *Religion and Science*. In it he warns us of the religion of fear that some people preach. He explains that to be good people we do not need someone to scare us by telling us that if we do not submit to him we will be in terrible pain for all eternity in a place called Hell.

Nor do we need someone to try to bribe us by offering us a wonderful reward, eternal life in heaven, if we obey. Einstein explained that *empathy and reason* should be the things that make us do what is right and what is good. Empathy will also keep us from harming others. We must always try to see things from different points of view, to seek understanding. *The motivation to be good must come from our inside not the outside.* Perhaps you should read that essay if you're curious.

If there is in fact a loving, heavenly Father he will be in many ways like normal, loving human parents are. He will try to care for us and protect us to the best of his ability. He will not try to scare us into obedience with ignorance and emotionalism.

Amaia, as a dad my love of your mom and you is unconditional. Helping, protecting and caring for you will always be my top priority. If there is a God I am sure he/she will understand the power of love.

There are three major religions in the part of the world you were born in. These are Christianity, Judaism and Islam. Christianity is by far the largest group in the US and Puerto Rico. As I said before, most of the people who believe in these religions are good people. I mentioned Jimmy Carter as an example of what I think a good believer should be.

However within these three groups there are smaller groups that are not very good at all. They are sometimes called fundamentalists. They feel that they, and they alone, are the *true* believers. They are very *intolerant* and they *do not allow questions or honest discussions* in their temples. They reject those who try to have open debates with them, sometimes violently. Fundamentalist Muslims, Jews and even Christians can be very hostile.

Fundamentalists have four main characteristics. They are theo-centric, dualistic, dogmatic and scriptural literalists. This means that they think that what they believe is God's only will.

They also see the world in dualistic terms, they are right and everybody else is wrong, they will be saved, everybody else won't and so on. There are no middle grounds. Dual means two. They only see two options in most things. Life is usually not that simple.

By dogmatic I mean that they fear questions and do not feel any obligation to provide reasons for their beliefs. Finally, they think that their sacred books are the only, unquestionable sources of divine and moral authority and whoever challenges *their* interpretation of their sacred book is an *infidel* or *apostate*. Perhaps you should look up the meaning of those two words later.

Never trust anyone who is afraid to answer your questions. Smart, honest and decent people do not fear questions. They welcome them.

As you grow older and you begin to understand the world a little better you will see what I mean. As you learn about history and science and you watch the news you will see that religion can sometimes be a force for unspeakable evil. There are other big religions in other parts of the world like India where many believe in Hinduism. All these people, Jews, Christians, Muslims and Hindus believe a million different things and they all claim to be right and to be the only true religion.

When the time comes you will make up your own mind. No need to rush anything. That will be your decision to make. Just remember, a good religion *brings people together*. It promotes love not hate, unity not separation, tolerance not intolerance, light not darkness. All these keep a good faith together. It does not use fear, ignorance and emotionalism to scare people into submission. Good people, believers or non-believers, are builders not destroyers.

Dear Amaia when it comes to issues of faith remember, *do not fear those who ask questions. Fear those who fear questions.* As Martin Luther King Jr., another famous Christian, once said: "Only light can drive away darkness. Only love can defeat hate." In this I believe as an agnostic, I believe in the power of love, knowledge and empathy.

About Science:

"Knowing *how* to think empowers you far beyond those who only know *what* to think."

Neil deGrasse Tyson

"Science is not perfect. It's often misused; it's only a tool, but *it's the best tool we have.* Self-correcting, ever changing, and applicable to everything: *with this tool we vanquish the impossible.*"

Carl Sagan

"I want to see." "I want to help you." "Why, Abu?" at age three and a half those were the three things you were constantly saying… constantly. One sunny afternoon in the summer of 2019 you and I went to our backyard for you to see some bees flying from flower to flower. There were hundreds of little purple flowers and dozens of bees getting pollen from them.

You were curious so I tried to explain how bees used pollen to make flowers grow and fruits possible. You started asking "Why, Abu?" I tried to explain the best that I could. Then I made a 'mistake'. I told you that bees made honey. I explained how *people* loved honey because it was such a great food.

"People eat food made by bees? Do they cook it for us?" you wanted to know. What could I do? Well, we went to the kitchen and I showed you a small bottle of honey. I gave you a bit of honey for you to taste. You liked it but now you wanted to know how the honey got into the bottle. Did the bees put it there? Well Amaia, there you have it. At age three you were already an amazing little scientist and your 'investigations' never ended...never... ha ha ha.

You were asking questions. You wanted to see, to help and know why things were the way they were. Ever since people are born they ask questions about everything. You were no different. *All things were new to you so you just needed to know*. Sadly, some adults do not like it when their children are constantly asking things. Some think children are meant to be seen not heard. That, I think, is a big mistake.

Asking questions is how we all grow. Richard Feynman, a famous American scientist, once said *he would rather have questions without answers than answers that could not be questioned.*

Science is all about asking questions, being *preguntón*. When people use science, they slowly improve their understanding of the world around them. This leads to technology that if used properly can improve our lives in many, many ways. Technology is the *application of science to solve practical problems*. For example, medical science can save lives. When I had my heart attack I was very near death. Thanks to science, a doctor in Mayaguez was able to repair my heart and almost four years later I am still around.

Thanks to science we also have intensive agriculture that allows many countries to feed their people. After many years of very hard work an incredible scientist called Norman Burlaug found the way to change plants so that they would produce more food for the people that needed it. Many consider him the father of something called the Green Revolution. Look it up when you can. His research and hard work helped feed millions of people in poor countries like India, Pakistan and Mexico. He once said, "Civilization as we know it today could not have evolved, nor can it survive, without an adequate food supply." I believe Burlaug was right.

If you open your fridge you'll probably see that the food we eat comes from all over the world. Oranges from Florida, strawberries from California, grapes from Chile and tuna fish from China. Boats, planes and trains make the cheap distribution of these foods possible. Thus millions can eat well without having to go hunting, fishing or planting things themselves. This is all made possible thanks to science and technology.

One thing that makes science such a great tool is that it's *self-correcting*. This means that *mistakes are a good thing in science* because we learn from them. You make experiments, you make mistakes, you make observations, you make changes and you move on. Good science, real science, is always changing and improving itself.

Another thing that makes science valuable is that it *forces people to give specific reasons for their claims*. In science you cannot just say something and expect others to believe you. You must provide independent, persuasive evidence for what you say.

The world, the cosmos, is so huge that people had to break its study into smaller chunks. In school you'll probably learn that there are many kinds of sciences. Some of the most important ones are biology, microbiology, chemistry, physics, geology, genetics, astronomy, mathematics and botany.

They all study different parts of nature. One looks at animals, another one looks at very small living things. Another science concentrates on plants or the stars, planets and galaxies. I will not go into details as to what each of these sciences does. That you will find out on your own as you grow older and get a better education.

For now I'll just give you some characteristics that all real sciences have in common. *Science is always **tentative.*** This means that you ask questions and find answers but those answers are not final. If in the future someone finds more, better information, you should change your mind.

Science is *always **evidence based***. This means that in science you never have to take anyone's words for anything. Everyone expects proof to support what is being said. People who do science must try to look at all the available evidence before forming an opinion.

Science *is also **honest***. This means that you must accept the possibility that you could be wrong. If this turns out to be the case, you must change your opinion. You will always respect the evidence above your initial ideas.

Science ***applies mostly to the physical world***. Thru science we understand a lot about how our planet works. The plants, the climate, the animals, the chemical and mineral elements and even the universe itself. All this can be understood when we use our brains to analyze and evaluate what we see in nature. As Sagan said, *science is not perfect*. Many people see it as a tool and that it is. But it is more than that. It is *by far the very best tool* humans have ever invented to understand life and our beautiful home, Earth. As Neil deGrasse Tyson pointed out, sciences is all about learning *how to think*. That's why it's so important that *young people like you* understand it and use it.

Finally, science is valuable because **it works**. People live longer and better lives when they use science. Countries that understand this and build their school curriculums around these facts create more peaceful, educated and prosperous societies. Their people are healthier and live longer. So even if you never become a scientist yourself you should understand how science works, why it's valuable and how we all benefit from it.

About Evil

"Ignorance, the root and stem of all evil."

Plato

"Overcome evil with love."

Bob Marley

I wish I did not have to speak about evil in a book dedicated to my young granddaughter but it is such a big part of so many people's lives that I cannot ignore it. Injustice, the biggest by-product of evil, is almost everywhere. Thanks to the Internet and Social Media, something happens on one side of the world and within minutes we can see it on our side of the planet. Smart phones, laptops and tablets make this possible. This is true about both the good and the bad. Evil can be present in the way people treat each other, the way many governments make their laws, the way some people do business and the way they treat our planet.

So, *what is evil?* Well, evil is when anyone *knowingly and willingly* uses his or her power to hurt others. Evil is present when, for no really good reason, someone uses violence, active or passive, to promote their own interests at the expense of others.

Most people think evil is easy to recognize and plain to see. We know, for example, that stealing from others is evil. If it's not yours don't take it. Pretty straightforward. Also, most of us know that hurting people, animals, or life in any of its many manifestations, is wrong. For example, some children deliberately cause pain to their pets, cats or dogs, for their entertainment. We adults must teach them that that is wrong. Sadly some adults do the same when they entertain themselves by watching bull fights or partaking in other blood 'sports' like dog or cock fights. In cases like these it's fairly easy to identify these acts as wrong, as evil.

Yet evil is not always that obvious. Sometimes those who commit evil simply change the words a bit to describe what they're doing in a different way. Suddenly, what was once so obviously wrong now seems acceptable or at least not so bad. After a while, after this word game has been going on for some time, it may even get to the point where what was once seen as terribly bad slowly becomes not only acceptable but downright necessary. George Orwell, the great English writer, once said: "Political language …is designed to make lies sound truthful and murder respectable, and to give an appearance of solidity to pure wind." What Orwell said is not only true of political language. It can be true of all kinds of language in which someone is trying to hide what they're really doing by changing words around. By changing some words they make it look like something other than what it really is. *Thus evil is often born when honesty dies.*

Such was the case of the colonization of the Americas by people like Christopher Columbus. When Columbus and other Europeans decided that they wanted to steal the land and resources of the so-called 'New' World, the Americas, they did not speak about theft or genocide, persecution or repression. No. They spoke about civilizing 'savages'. They spoke about doing away with 'inferior' cultures. The Europeans lusted for the gold, the minerals and the lands that belonged to others but they never once admitted what their true desires were because that would be to admit they were... well, evil.

Another example of evil is evident in what is commonly called the Fossil Fuel Industry. These are big, big companies that produce energy by finding, refining and selling products made of petroleum, coal and natural gas. These products give us useful things like gasoline for our vehicles, electricity for our homes and many more things like plastics and heating oil that keeps many homes warm in winter.

The trouble is that most of these companies have known for decades, since at least the 1970s, that when these fuels are used in our cars, trucks, planes or power plants they threw tons of CO2 into the atmosphere. This is a greenhouse gas that makes the planet warmer and warmer. This in turn causes something terrible called *Climate Change*. The ice in the polar caps is melting and the whole planet is rapidly getting warmer.

This change in the climate puts billions of living beings in danger. The weather swings to terrible extremes. In 2018 while the states in the northeast of the United States were becoming unbelievably cold, minus 40 degrees Fahrenheit in Chicago, in Australia, on the other side of the world, it was getting so hot that the asphalt roads were melting and birds were falling from the sky and dying. From violent hurricanes in the Atlantic Ocean to terrible droughts in parts of Asia, the weather has become increasingly unpredictable and extreme.

By hiding this important information from the people and governments of the world the Fossil Fuel Industry became evil. They put their profits, making money, above the long term wellbeing of the people and even the whole planet.

But there is hope. You may like to know that a young girl, much like you, is at the front of the struggle to save the planet from greed and pollution. Her name is Greta Thunberg and she's from Sweden. All around the world hundreds of thousands of young people marched and protested in favor of the environment. In one protest she led 1.4 million students from 112 countries to protest for climate change legislation to protect the environment. They demanded that adults stop talking and start doing something to save the planet. She is a very brave young lady who is working to save the world from human greed and stupidity.

When you were barely 3 years old, evil also raised its very ugly head in the US. Thousands of mainly very poor, desperate people, traveled thousands of miles to escape their home countries in Central and South America. They were trying to escape poor countries torn apart by drug violence, terrible lack of stability and little opportunities for themselves and their loved ones. They traveled, mostly on foot, thousands of miles from places like Honduras, Guatemala, Mexico, El Salvador and other poor countries. They thought that in the US they could find help, maybe even asylum and a better life. It did not turn out that way.

When these poor people finally arrived to our southern border they were received with terrible hostility. Their children were forcefully taken away from their families. As of March of 2019 hundreds of these children were now missing and their families were destroyed by this massive kidnapping of innocent kids by the federal government in charge of protecting our southern border.

Hundreds of kids and adults were arrested and put in detention centers where they were treated like criminals when all they wanted was the chance to apply for political asylum. Some adults were even forced to go back home without their children.

This is evil. The truly sad part is that many of those who were not directly affected by this terrible abuse of power were completely indifferent to these terrible crimes. This general silence reminded me of something Dr. Martin Luther King Jr. once said. "In the end it is not the words of our enemies that we remember but the silence of our friends."

Now, evil need not be something big like the colonization of the Americas more than 500 years ago or the destruction of our planet by the actions of the Fossil Fuel Industry or the kidnapping of poor children in our border with Mexico.

Evil can also be personal, seemingly small. When we see someone who speaks a language we do not understand, or dressed differently we may feel tempted to make fun of them, reject them or even bully them. Sadly, some people, bullies, can only feel good about themselves by making others feel bad. This makes them feel superior to those they are attacking. This too is evil. Under no circumstances should we ever seek to hurt others just to make ourselves feel that we are somehow better than they are. NUNCA.

This brings me to what I think you need to understand. Never let anyone fool you into accepting evil by changing its name to make it seem acceptable. Never stop thinking for yourself. If someone or something is needlessly getting hurt, do not go along with those who are committing evil. Raise your voice when needed. Speak your truth. Indifference, more than anything else, feeds evil and wrong doing.

Someone once wrote that *a rose by any other name is still a rose*. That wonderful principal applies to most things in life, good and bad. Slavery is slavery no matter how much you want to hide it by calling it something else. Sexism and racism are still awful things even when some people want to make them seem 'good' by calling them something else.

Trust your intuition and take a good long look at the results of people's actions before going along with anything. There is a lot of evil in the world but there are also many good people trying to make the world a better place. I sincerely hope you will always try very hard to be one of those people. We must always try to protect ourselves and those around us from the forces of evil, wherever we may find them, even within ourselves.

About your Roots and your Culture:

"Puerto Rico's a beautiful place and *puertorriqueños* are a beautiful race."

NY Poet Pedro Pietri

"Yo sería borincano, aunque naciera en la luna."

Poet Juan Antonio Corretjer

Amaia, you were born in Puerto Rico. Most of your family has its roots in the northwestern part of the island. Puerto Rico is one of the most beautiful places on Earth. It has warm, tropical weather all year long and many people who come as visitors end up staying. It has world class beaches and restaurants and lovely, warm and welcoming people.

The beaches of Isabela, Aguadilla and Rincón are world renowned by surfers who come from all over the planet to ride their waves. I lived for years in a place called Ramey, a former Air Force base, in Aguadilla. In 2016 I could drive around Ramey and see two things on many cars. Surf boards and out of state license plates. Plates from Florida, California, New Jersey, New York, Nevada and other far away states were very common. Especially in the winter months, from November to February, thousands of northerners would come down to vacation in Puerto Rico to get away from the terrible northern cold. However, beautiful beaches and warm weather are not the only things going for Puerto Rico.

For such a small country Puerto Rico has also been the home or roots of many, many outstanding people in almost all areas of human activities. Literature, politics, science, sports, music and cinema, to name a few, are areas in which Puerto Ricans have more than their fair share of excellent representation. There are many more than those I mention here but I don't need to name them all to make my point. There is much to be proud of when it comes to your cultural heritage.

In 2016, the year you were born, there were three Boricuas taking the world by storm due to their enormous talent and hard work. Lin-Manuel Miranda, Monica Puig and Lauri Hernandez. These three young Puerto Ricans were recognized as the best of the best in their fields by the whole planet.

Let's start with Lin-Manuel Miranda. This young man wrote, directed and acted in a Broadway play called *Hamilton*. This play became one of Broadway's greatest hits ever. Ticket sales were unheard of and many people thought Hamilton was one of the best American plays in many years. Tickets were selling so fast that people had to buy them months or even years in advance.

Broadway, just so you know, is the center of the universe when it comes to American plays. It is in New York City and they say that if you can make it there you can make it anywhere. Well, Lin-Manuel, a Puerto Rican kid from NYC, made it there in a big way. But Broadway wasn't the only place Lin-Manuel was successful in.

Early in 2017 a song Lin-Manuel wrote for the animated movie *Moana* was nominated for an Oscar. This is the prize they give to the best movies every year. *How Far I'll Go* didn't get the Oscar but it was still a great accomplishment.

In most countries, outstanding work is usually celebrated with special awards. When it comes to the US it goes like this. In movies it's the Oscar. In news and journalism it's the Pulitzer Prize, in music it's the Grammy and in theater it's the Tony Award. By age 37 Lin-Manuel had earned two Grammy Awards, one Pulitzer Prize and three Tony Awards. So, I wouldn't be surprised if you knew him way before you read these lines.

Monica Puig is another outstanding Boricua. During the 2016 Olympic Games in Brazil she became the very first Puerto Rican to win an Olympic gold medal for Puerto Rico. She played against the best tennis players the world had to offer and one by one she beat them all. The whole island was full of pride for her accomplishment.

Monica grew up in the USA and she worked very hard to become a world class athlete. Monica showed the whole world what a young Puerto Rican woman could do if she set her heart to it.

Last, but definitely not least, we had Laurie Hernandez. This young lady represented the USA in gymnastics in the same Olympics in Rio de Janeiro, Brazil and she won gold and silver medals for the American Olympic team. She went on to compete in other events such as *Dancing with the Stars*, a popular television dancing competition, and she also won there. When you were a baby these three young Boricuas were showing the world what Puerto Ricans were capable of doing, but they were by no means the first ones. Because there are so many other stars like them I will only mention a few in each field.

The point I want to make is simple. You may someday run into some people, some very ignorant people, who know nothing about Puerto Rico and may want to make you feel like being Boricua is somehow a bad thing.

They may have their minds full of ignorance, prejudice and maybe even hate. Do not listen to them and *never allow anyone to define you based on their ignorance*. As a Puerto Rican you are no better nor worse than anybody else. There is much to be proud of in your Caribbean heritage.

Keep in mind that as a Boricua you are in fact a *fifth generation American* because the people of Puerto Rico have been American citizens since 1917, 98 years before you were born. So *you are not a foreigner in the US and neither is your family.* When a Puerto Rican family moves from the island to a state it's the same as a New Yorker moving to Texas or California.

You are not an immigrant. Puerto Ricans have been an important part of the USA for well over a century. They also have a proud military tradition. They have protected and served in the US Armed Forces since the year 1899, eighteen years before they even became US citizens. Since that time over 330 thousand Boricuas have served as veterans and as of 2017 there were more than 35 thousand Puerto Ricans in active duty. These numbers do not include the thousands that are spread over the 50 states serving in the Army/Air Force National Guard units.

The *65th of Infantry* is an Army Unit that was mostly made up of Puerto Rican soldiers and they were among the most con-decorated soldiers in US history. The Borinqueneers, as they were known, were brave defenders of the US of A for decades. What follow are some examples of outstanding Puerto Ricans in many other fields.

Cinema:

José Ferrer: He was the first Puerto Rican to become a major star in Hollywood and he was also the first one to earn an Oscar, American cinema's biggest prize. In 1947 he got the Tony Award for his outstanding acting in a play called *Cyrano de Bergerac*. A few years later, in 1950, he got an Oscar for his acting in the movie *Cyrano de Bergerac*, the Hollywood adaptation of the same play. The first Puerto Rican and Hispanic for that matter to achieve such honors.

Rita Moreno: She is also a major Hollywood movie star and is the first woman to have won an Oscar, a Tony and a Grammy. These are the three most important prizes in American popular arts. Her Oscar was for best supporting actress in the musical *West Side Story* (1962). In 1972 she won a Grammy and in 1975 a Tony Award. Finally in 1977 she got an Emmy Award for an outstanding TV series performance.

Benicio del Toro: Benicio is another amazing actor who has been all over the place in popular

American movies for decades. He started in the late 1980's with small bad guy roles in TV shows like *Miami Vice* and slowly worked his way into Hollywood movies. In 1988 he played a supporting role in *Big Top Pee-Wee*, a children's comedy movie. Then he landed roles in a James Bond movie, *A License to Kill* (1989), *The Usual Suspects* (1995), *The Fan* (1996), opposite mega star Robert De Niro and has been acting in great movies ever since. In 2014 he had a supporting role in mega hit *Guardians of the Galaxy* and was later cast in the greatest movie franchise of all times *Star Wars*, in 2017, when you were only little over a year old, Benicio played a bad guy in *Star Wars: The Last Jedi*.

Raul Julia: The great Raul Julia was until his death one of Hollywood's most respected actors. He could do anything, from comedies to intense political dramas, truly an actor's actor. He stared in movies such as *Romero, The Adams Family, The Burning Season* and many, many others. Although he died very young, his place in American cinema history is assured due to the quantity and quality of his work. I mention here only a small part of his legacy. Check it out when you can.

Jimmy Smit: Jimmy Smit is an excellent actor who has enjoyed success in both TV dramas and Hollywood movies. He has played both lead roles and supporting roles. In 2016 Smit even had a supporting role in *Rouge One* the Star Wars movie that came out on your birth year, the only Boricua in this great movie's cast. Jimmy was no stranger to the Star Wars movies however. In 2002 he acted in *Star Wars: Episode II*, then in *Attack of the Clones* (2005), and *Revenge of the Sith*. Benicio del Toro eventually joined Jimmy in the cast of *The Last Jedi*.

Music:

Rafael Hernández: He was one of the greatest composers of the early XX century. His music may be old, but like George Gershwin's, it is timeless. He wrote such classics as *Lamento Borincano* and *Campanitas de Cristal*. He was very famous in Puerto Rico and the whole world during my father's life time. I remember listening to his wonderful music on my father's record player when I was a child. Sadly, most younger people do not know of his music. You can hear and sometimes see him in some old movies in YouTube videos.

It is important for you to keep in mind that there is more than 100 years' worth of sound and video recordings of wonderful music from all parts of the world. Open your ears and heart to all of the sounds and sights of all these wonderful artists from different generations. I am sure your generation will also produce great music.

Ricky Martin: Ricky is the ultimate pop star. He started his career with a local boy band called *Menudo* and later went on to solo fame and glory. He has had many hits in both Spanish and English. But Ricky is more than just a pop star. He is heavily involved in saving children from all kinds of abuse with his organization the Ricky Martin Foundation. It educates people and actively protects children from abuse. Thousands of kids have been saved thanks to his wonderful work. His mega hit *Livin la Vida Loca* was all over the media when it came out in the 1990's and he has been recording hits ever since.

Mark Anthony: An outstanding singer from NYC who can do pop, salsa and ballads. He is also a successful actor with credits in both Hollywood movies and TV shows. His career includes singing, acting, producing and even entrepreneurship, with more than a few successful business ventures. He is best known for his great salsa music. His *Todo a Su Tiempo* album (1995) put him on the musical map and he was still a major star in 2017. I'll leave it to you to check out his work if you like.

El Gran Combo: This is the greatest salsa band of all times. Salsa is a kind of music that was born in Cuba and later moved to NYC and Puerto Rico. It is a festive music with trumpets, pianos, congas and other instruments. Their career lasted over 50 years and they recorded dozens of successful albums. *Los mulatos del sabor* have represented Puerto Rican music all over the world. Salsa was created in the late 1960's between New York City and Puerto Rico. Major acts include *Ritchy Ray and Bobby Cruz*, la *Fania All Stars*, *La Sonora Ponseña*, *La Selecta*, Hector Lavoe, Tito Puente, Celia Cruz, Ruben Blades and Ismael Miranda.

Jennifer López: Like Rita Moreno, J-Lo seems to be capable of doing everything. She is successful in music, acting, dancing and business. Not many artists, male or female, can move from one art form to another and be successful in all those fields. Jennifer is a Boricua from Queens, New York who has been successful doing just that for decades now.

José Feliciano: José, a poor blind kid from Lares, Puerto Rico, who's family moved to New York City when he was very young. As a child growing up in NYC, José was surrounded by all kinds of music. He listened to Latin music, blues, rock, classical, jazz, Broadway, trio music, soul and Boricua *jíbaro* music. José took all those sounds to heart and learned how to play the guitar. Being blind meant that he spent most of his time in an apartment with his family. With a lot of practice and determination José Feliciano became one of the world's best guitar players. The man could play anything. You name it and he could do it. I don't know if YouTube will be around when you grow up but if it is, check him out playing *Flight of the Bumble Bee*, *La Malagueña* and *Que Será*, one of his all-time classics. Come Christmas you will hear *Feliz Navidad*, another of his compositions, all over the place.

Bruno Mars: This young man, Peter Gene Hernández, is a major pop music star. Already in 2016 he had sold nearly 100 million copies of his music albums. He combines Latin music, blues, jazz, r&b and hip hop to produce wonderful pop music that is loved by millions around the world.

By 2016 he had won a total of four Grammies and was just getting started when you came to us.

Luis Fonsi and Daddy Yankee: In the summer of 2017 a song by these two Boricua stars took the world by storm. *Despacito,* became the year's monster hit. From Europe to Latin America to Africa and Asia the song was everywhere. These two were a musical odd couple. Fonsi is a romantic ballad singer while Daddy Yankee is an urban reggeaton artist. Yet oddly the song worked. While many people in Asia and Europe didn't understand the lyrics because they were in Spanish, they enjoyed the melody and the festive video. By early July the YouTube video had an incredible two and a half BILLION views (2,472,487,259 views) and was well on its way to becoming one of the most successful music videos of all time. Even your beloved minions made a great cover of the popular song.

Sports:

Roberto Clemente: Number 21 of the Pittsburg Pirates, was one of the greatest baseball players of all time. He was a native of Carolina, Puerto Rico and was a role model for the young all over the world. But Roberto Clemente was more than just a baseball player. He also worked very hard helping others in need. When a big earthquake hit the poor country of Nicaragua in the early 1970s Roberto volunteered to take food, clothing and medicine to the victims of the disaster. Sadly, the plane he was in crashed shortly after leaving San Juan. He and his companions died in the accident. But Clemente's humanitarian legacy lives on.

Yet Clemente was not alone. He was just one of many outstanding baseball players. As I was writing these lines Ivan Rodriguez, another great ball player, became the fourth Boricua to be added the Baseball Hall of Fame. The list of great Puerto Rican ball players is too long for me to mention here. If you're ever curious do a bit of research my dear.

Baseball is America's and Puerto Rico's pastime and towards the end of March, on the 22nd, Puerto Rico's baseball team participated in the *2017 World Baseball Classic*. This was a world class event that was seen by hundreds of millions of fans from all over the planet. Outstanding teams from all over the world came to compete. Japan, the Netherlands, Cuba, the USA, Puerto Rico and many other nations faced each other. They met in California, USA.

The whole island came to a standstill to watch *Team Rubio* play world class baseball. At the end they lost only one game to reach second place in the world sports event to the US team. Ironically, the US pitcher that finally defeated PR was also a Puerto Rican, Marcus Stroman, who became the tournament's most valuable player. It took a Boricua to stop the Boricuas, what an incredible sporting event.

Gigi Fernández: She was an amazing tennis player who represented the US in the Olympics earning a gold medal with her team. She won an amazing 17 Grand Slam titles, two Olympic gold medals for the US team and she was ranked for a time as the number one woman's double tennis player in the whole world. Another Boricua woman who was a role model for many others after her.

Hector 'El Macho' Camacho: Camacho was only one of many, many great Puerto Rican boxers. He won three world championships. But he was not alone. To name a few, Tito Trinidad also got three world championships, Wilfredo Benitez also earned three championships and the great Miguel Cotto won an incredible four championships. I never liked boxing very much but we must acknowledge the impact that Boricua fighters have had on that sport. The videos of their fights and accomplishments are probably available on line for you to see.

Literature:

Piri Thomas: He was the writer of the classic Boricua-American novel *Down These Mean Streets*. It spoke about the life of a poor Puerto Rican kid in the heart of New York City. A very strong and realistic story of life in el Barrio, describing the good and bad things of living in urban poverty.

Jesús Colón: Jesús was one of the very first Boricua writers to speak about what it was like to be a Puerto Rican in the United States in the early XX century. He got to New York City in 1918, nearly a hundred years before you were born and was a very smart and sensitive man. His warm and insightful essays are a window to a world long gone but sadly many of the problems Jesús spoke about so long ago are still with us. His masterpiece and a favorite book of mine was *A Puerto Rican in New York,* a collection of personal and touching essays of his fight to belong to a society that often rejected him on two counts. He was Puerto Rican and he was black, not a good combination in the eyes of some who hate. Colón was the father of the Newyorican Writers Movement. These were stateside Boricuas who wrote poetry, short stories, essays and plays in English about the Puerto Rican experiences in the USA. I considered myself part of that literary tradition.

Enrique Laguerre: In 1935 Laguerre, a native from Moca, your maternal grandmother's home town, published a book titled *La Llamarada*. This novel described the very hard life of people in the sugarcane plantations. It was really a form of slavery. The novel is a masterpiece. Someone once said that if we want to know history we should read history books but if we want to live history we should read literature. *La Llamarada* is that kind of book, a book that allows you to live the pain and hardship of poor people trying to survive in a cruel and abusive economic system. Another outstanding book by Laguerre is *La Resaca*. These are two must reads to understand the Puerto Rico of the early XX century.

Esmeralda Santiago: She is also an outstanding writer whose greatest work is a book titled *When I was Puerto Rican.* She wrote about her experiences not only as a Puerto Rican in the states but as a woman who sometimes had to face discrimination due to her gender and her culture. As a young Puerto Rican woman this is a novel you may want to read some day.

Law

Sonia Sotomayor: This amazing woman grew up poor in the Bronx, in New York City and thru hard work and dedication made it all the way to the US Supreme Court. This court is the one that has the final word on issues that affect the whole country. She is the first Hispanic woman to sit in the highest court of the land. She graduated Magna Cum Laude from Princeton University in 1976 and in 1979 also got a law degree from Yale University. These, by the way, are two of the most prestigious universities in the world.

Her dad, an alcoholic factory worker, died when she was only 9 years old but her mom, a very strong and determined woman, raised her. Sonia always had an intense love for books, learning and education. She also had a great work ethic and all this paid off in a big way. Sonia's life has not been easy. She has battled health issue like diabetes but has achieved her goals in life. An amazing role model in many ways.

Alexandría Ocasio-Cortes: This young Puerto Rican New Yorker is making history by the week. She became the youngest woman ever elected to the US Congress when she beat Republican Anthony Papas. Before that she defeated Joe Crowley, a Democrat veteran NY politician who had served ten terms. Alexandría worked as a waitress and a bartender before running for Congress and winning in the 2018 mid-term elections. She has rocked the boat in Washington by proposing a number of seemingly controversial laws or bills. These include the Green New Deal, the 70% marginal tax rate beyond the first 10 million dollars of income, Medicare for All, free college education at state universities and the Federal Job Guarantee Bill. While some of these bills may be controversial for some there is no question that Alexandría is becoming a force to be dealt with in Washington DC. She is a great example of what determination, intelligence and education can mean for a woman who is not afraid to speak her mind and work towards her goals with determination and passion. You may want to look her up on the Internet and watch some of her speeches. AOC, as she is also known, is a great public speaker and a fine role model for young women everywhere.

Science:

Niel Degrass Tyson: Niel, whose mother is Puerto Rican, is one of a small group of celebrity scientists that is well known and respected the world over. These scientists made science fun and understandable to people who were not scientists. He's an astrophysicist and a hardcore promoter of science and reason. He hosted a 2015 science TV series called *Cosmos: A Space Time Odyssey*. This 13 episode science program was based on an original show first aired in the early 1980s. That original program was created by Degrass Tyson's mentor and teacher Carl Sagan. I know your mom loved this series and I hope she shares it with you one day. Sagan's version was one of my favorite shows when I was a younger.

Pedro Rodriguez: Dr. Rodriguez is a scientist, an inventor and a mechanical engineer. After the Space Shuttle Columbia was destroyed in a tragic accident involving a booster rocket failure Dr. Rodriguez led a team of scientists chosen to fix the problem and that they did. Thanks to their work the space shuttle program was able to fly again for many years.

Dr. Ricardo Alegría: He was an anthropologist, a historian and an archeologist. He was the director of the *Instituto de Cultura Puertoriqueña*, the Puerto Rican Institute of Culture. Many people think that Dr. Alegría singlehandedly saved the *Viejo San Juan* from the efforts to 'modernize' the old colonial city by destroying all the old buildings. He was also a fierce protector of all things related to Puerto Rican culture. He rescued our Taino cultural heritage by protecting the Taino sites that were discovered all over the island and made us more aware of our history as a people.

Dr. Monserrate Roman: This is an amazing scientist. Her research goals were to find ways to control the environment within the International Space Station and keep the scientists alive and healthy as they lived for months in outer space. She's a microbiologist and she and her team controlling the life support system of the station. Her work with NASA, *National Aeronautics and Space Association*, was vital in protecting the lives all the people up there in orbit in space around our planet. Without a safe living environment there could be no space missions.

Dr. Yahaira Sierra Sastre: She's another outstanding scientist from Cornell University. She is a doctor in nano-technology and she was part of a program called HI-SEAS, "Hawaiian Space Exploration Analog and Simulation. She studied the effects of extreme isolation on astronauts and its effect on their eating habits and health. Dr. Sierra even took part in a program in which a group of scientists were isolated in a closed environment that simulated a space station. From March 2013 to August 2013 they were closed in that environment to see how their bodies reacted. This gave them information that allowed them to make better and safer space vehicles.

Joseph Michael "Joe" Acabá: Dr. Acabá is a NASA hydro-geologist who became the very first Puerto Rican astronaut. He spent several hours in a historical space walk in which he helped repair solar power devices that generated energy for the International Space Station. Proud of his roots, he carried a small Puerto Rican flag in his travel to space. Joseph started his career as a science teacher at a public High School in California. This young man of science surely stands as a great role model, showing the world what a strong work ethic and a desire to be successful can do for you.

As I said earlier, there are many, many other outstanding Puerto Ricans doing wonderful things around the world and making life better for themselves and so many others. These are just a small sample of what a Boricua such as you can do with your life if you are willing to work hard and smart. Never stop learning my dear and never stop growing.

Perhaps XIX century intellectual Eugenio Maria de Hostos said it best when he wrote that the only way for one to become useful to ideas and people is to *raise men (and women) to discuss their duties instead of lowering them to negotiate their interests.* When smart, decent people work hard to help others everybody benefits.

About Spanish:

Querida Amaia, el español es el idioma de tu gente, el de tus abuelos, tus padres y toda tu familia. El leer y escribirlo bien es importante de mil maneras distintas. Para comenzar, si dominas el español podrás comunicarte efectivamente con la enorme mayoría de la gente del mundo. El español, junto al inglés, son los dos idiomas *internacionales* más usados en todo el planeta.

El idioma número uno de todo el mundo es el chino mandarín, pero ese es el idioma de una sola gran nación, China. El español por su parte es hablado en muchos países al igual que el inglés. Por ejemplo, México, Puerto Rico, España, Argentina, Cuba, Venezuela, Costa Rica y muchos otros países hablan español. El inglés es hablado en Inglaterra, Jamaica, Irlanda, Escocia, los Estados Unidos y Australia entre otros.

Cuando hablas español mantienes contacto con tus raíces. Te puedes entender mejor con la familia que por una razón u otra solo habla ese idioma. El ser bilingüe también te permite disfrutar de tantas cosas lindas que nacen de nuestra herencia puertorriqueña. Puedes disfrutar mejor de la música, los libros, las películas y las ideas que vienen de nuestra isla. Puedes comunicarte mejor con toda tu familia en la isla, tu sangre y tu cultura.

Al ser también un idioma Internacional, puedes entender y apreciar las culturas de muchas naciones. En términos educativos y profesionales es muy ventajoso hablar *al menos* dos idiomas. Muchos empleos requieren que uno trabaje con gente que habla distintos idiomas y el saberlos te da grandes ventajas sobre los que solo pueden hablar una sola lengua.

De hecho, en casi todos los lugares del mundo el ser bilingüe es lo normal. La mayoría de la gente habla dos o más idiomas. Esto es cierto en muchos de los países de Europa. En lugares como Finlandia, Suecia, Holanda se hablan varios idiomas. Lo mismo ocurre en Asia y en África.

Penosamente alguna gente en los EUA no entiende esto y rechaza cualquier idioma que no sea el inglés. Favorecen lo que ellos llaman *English Only*. Esto es absurdo y debes cuidarte de esta actitud de mentes chiquitas. El ser bilingüe es mucho mejor que hablar solamente un idioma.

Además, mucha gente desconoce que el español ha sido desde el mismo principio parte importante de la historia de los Estados Unidos. Se puede ver en los nombres de muchos lugares. Nevada, Florida, Montana, Los Ángeles, El Paso, San Agustín son algunos ejemplos de lugares de EUA con nombres en español. La cuidad más antigua de los Estados Unidos está en Florida y se llama San Agustín. Hasta tiene un pequeño 'castillo' muy parecido al Morro del Viejo San Juan y su primer idioma fue durante muchos años el español.

El estado de Texas, uno de los más grandes y ricos de la nación, era hasta mediados del siglo XIX parte de México, un país hispano-parlante. Así que no hay nada de extranjero en lo que al español se refiere en los EUA. En el caso de Puerto Rico, nosotros no venimos a los Estados Unidos. En 1898 los Estados Unidos vinieron a nosotros cuando el General Miles invadió la isla en la Guerra Hispano-Americana.

Además, el bilingüismo tiene otras ventajas. La gente bilingüe tiende a ser más inteligente y más ágiles y rápidos en la resolución de problemas. Con un segundo idioma uno no solo adquiere acceso a otra manera de comunicarse, sino que también consigue entrar en otras culturas, literaturas, músicas, poesías e historias. La gente plenamente bilingüe, las que domina las cuatro artes del lenguaje, *entender, hablar, leer y escribir*, puede ver el mundo desde muchos puntos de vista, muchas perspectivas, y esto es algo muy bueno. Generalmente mientras más información uno tiene acerca de un asunto mejor lo entiende.

También, la persona bilingüe puede leer las grandes obras en el idioma en que fueron creadas. Cervantes, Unamuno, y las tremendas obras de la literatura boricua pueden ser leídas y disfrutadas en su idioma original. *La Charca* de Manuel Zeno Gandia, *El Jíbaro* de Manuel A. Alonso o *La Carreta* de René Marqués todas deben ser leídas, si es posible en español, el idioma en el que nacieron.

En fin, de todo corazón espero que crezcas amando y usando al menos dos idiomas para que tu mundo sea más rico y feliz. Es más, no te tienes que limitar a solo dos idiomas. Aprende todos los idiomas que puedas. Esto te expondrá a un mundo mucho más grande. Como dijera un sabio alguna vez, *"Los límites de mi idioma son los límites de mi mundo."* Nunca seas menos de lo que puedes ser. Jamás te limites.

About Hurricane María:

When Mother Nature gets angry and starts throwing things around there is very little humans can do to stop her. On September of 2017 she was extremely pissed off and she was coming to the Caribbean.

Originally I had no intention of speaking about hurricanes in your book but since this event took place before I had finished the final draft I decided to include it. This particular hurricane was the strongest one to hit Puerto Rico in almost a hundred years so it was of great historical significance.

On September 20th Hurricane María, a near Category 5 storm, hit Puerto Rico and you Amaia were there. Hurricanes are divided into different groups depending on how big and strong they are. The weaker ones are category 1 and they go up from there. The stronger the storm the higher the number, five being the strongest, most dangerous category.

Well, María was, according to most experts, a Cat 5. She was very angry indeed and she was definitely throwing things. When she came into Puerto Rico she had sustained winds of nearly 175 miles an hour, mph, and gusts of almost 200 mph. She moved slowly across the island taking almost 23 hours to cross it from one side to the other.

In less than a day María changed the lives of millions of people. By the time this thing left Puerto Rico it had effectively destroyed our grid. What's a grid? Well, glad you asked. A grid is the system that society creates to serve its needs most effectively.

You want food? You go to the supermarket and buy vegetables and fruits. You may even get good food by simply opening your fridge. You need not go to a farm. Just go into your kitchen and look for the place where all the food comes from. Read the labels and you'll see something amazing. You'll see that much of your food has traveled hundreds if not thousands of miles to get to your home.

Need water? Well, you open the faucet and there it is. You want it cold? Just open the freezer and get some ice cubes.

You need power for your microwave, your TV, your laptop or your stove? All you have to do is flick a switch and all the power you need is right there in the form of electricity. You have roads, vehicles, instant communication and so many other things. Thanks to these roads and vehicles you can move from point A to point B rapidly, cheaply and safely. Thanks to phones you can speak to anyone in the next town, the next country or on the other side of the planet in a matter of seconds. All these things made up a grid that took many, many years to build.

Well, mean old María took all that away from Puerto Rico in a few short hours. Many Boricua families lost running water and electricity for months. Thousands of families even lost their homes. Wooden houses with metal roofs did not stand a chance with María. Their roofs were literally blown away and twisted beyond recognition. Hundreds of houses that were near rivers or on the beach were destroyed or badly damaged. Eventually the number of homes destroyed by Hurricane María would approach 200 thousand. That was 200 thousand families who suddenly became homeless due to no fault of their own.

Many roads were covered with trees, mud and branches. Tons of material needed to be removed slowly and often painfully. Swollen rivers washed away bridges and roads. Mud slides made it impossible for people to use their cars because the roads were now blocked. Mountain towns like Utuado, Yauco, Jayuya and Barranquitas were isolated for many days from the rest of the island. For the first few days helicopters were used to drop food and supplies for the people there.

The strong winds destroyed thousands of miles of power lines leaving most of Puerto Rico in the dark for many months. Candles and flashlights were suddenly the most valuable things you could have come sundown. You, my dear, learned the word 'flashlight' just a few days after María had passed. We would show you one and you would, to our delight, say the word over and over again. Ha, ha...

Before María struck I was very worried about you and your mom's safety so I asked her to stay with me during the storm. She agreed.

As luck would have it, hurricane María left the island very near Aguadilla giving us a double whammy. Since the eye of the storm passed over our town we got hit with the wind moving violently in one direction for many hours and then, a second time, from the other direction, again for many hours.

As I said before, this was no ordinary storm. This was a once in a lifetime event. The last one of this size to hit the island dated back to the late 1920's, San Felipe, nearly a hundred years earlier. One of my strongest images of that frightening day was seeing you standing up on my bed looking out a window saying 'Bahh' in your innocent surprise as your exhausted mother lay down next to you trying to rest a bit. You were about a year and eight months old at the time so you were still a baby.

Our house was a very strong, well-built cement brick home, so we were safe from the savage storm that was rocking the world outside. Little did we know that the real effects of María's visit would only be felt after she left our lovely island.

When we were finally able to leave the house safely we found a brand new world had begun in Puerto Rico. All the things we took for granted for so many years were now gone. No more grid. Clean water was hard to come by and it was not coming out of our faucets. We had to collect rain water to flush toilets and wash our clothing by hand. We also needed be very careful with the water we drank because contaminated water was very dangerous. During the weeks after the storm drinking dirty water made many people very sick and some even died.

The lines for buying gasoline for our cars were six and seven hours long and stretched for miles. We would get up at 3:30 am to get in line with our cars so that maybe we could buy some gas, a very limited amount, by noon. Supermarkets were almost empty and the government had places called Oasis where we would stand in line for hours with empty one gallon jugs so we could fill them up with clean water. During those first weeks after the storm we survived one day at a time by getting up very early and doing whatever lines were needed to make it thru that one day.

Even going to the bank was a struggle. One day your uncle Kevin and I spent seven hours in line at the Aguadilla Mall bank to get just one hundred dollars from my banking account. Initially the banks would not allow us to take more than $100 no matter how much money we had there.

People were starting to get very sick and many hospitals did not have enough medicine, doctors or the medical equipment to care for them. We realized that you, your mom and my mother needed to go somewhere safer. So my sister, who lived in Jacksonville, and I arranged to get you three to Florida as soon as possible. There you would be safer. After a lot of hard work on the phone we were able to get airplane tickets out of the island. But we weren't the only ones trying to leave Puerto Rico.

Hurricane María caused a mass exodus of Boricua families who moved mostly to Florida and some to Texas, New York and other states. In just a few weeks more than a 200 thousand people left everything they had in Puerto Rico and moved to Florida where they could find better jobs and more opportunities for themselves and their children. Some estimated that within the first seven weeks after the storm nearly half a million people had left the island. Many had left only for a while. They would return as soon as the crisis passed. This was especially true of the elderly. Others would remain in their new stateside homes.

It was a very sad time because most of those who moved away left loved ones behind and it is never easy to say goodbye to someone you love. Leaving the island was something most people did because they felt they had no choice at the moment.

Besides, Puerto Rico is such an amazing island. Even after the damage a hurricane of this size caused, the island still remained one of the most beautiful places you can imagine. Sadly, some scientists said that it would take about 40 years for the vegetation to regain its pre-Maria abundance and health. Yet the storm could not take away the beauty of *Borinquen Bella*.

I really didn't want you, your mom and my mother, who was about 82 at the time, to be so far away but *when you love somebody you always try to do what is best for them*. It broke my heart yet I knew you three would all be much safer up north than in Puerto Rico. We all thought at the time that it was the right thing to do.

My job and some health issues required that I stay in Puerto Rico. But as I said before, doing what we need to do instead of what we want to do is never an easy task.

The job of rebuilding Puerto Rico started immediately after the hurricane was over. Thousands of Puerto Ricans took to the streets and started cleaning things up. Government workers, both local and many from other states, came to our rescue. Volunteers from Texas, Florida, Georgia and even Alaska found their way to Puerto Rico and gave of their time and skills to get our island on its feet again.

Military personnel, Army, Airforce and Navy were everywhere. Large planes came in around the clock with supplies from many different places with food, water, equipment of all kinds. Living in Ramey, a former Air Force base, allowed Kevin and I to literally see and hear these planes and choppers taking off and landing constantly. Most of these soldiers were in fact Puerto Ricans who were working to rescue their own island and families from the wrath of María. At one point there were about 72 military helicopters and more than 15 thousand soldiers all over Puerto Rico helping communities recover.

When most of the military left in mid-November, General Jeffrey S. Buchanan reported that they had opened 3,400 miles of roads, distributed 51 million bottles of water, served 20 million meals, distributed 4 million gallons of bulk water, treated more than 5,000 patients and restored cell phone communications in at least nine locations.

Many civilian volunteers were also everywhere. Even famous artists like Mark Anthony, J-Lo, Lin-Manuel Miranda, Ricky Martin and many others organized concerts to raise money for the victims of María. Many stateside Americans were also very generous with their time and money when it came to lending Puerto Rico a hand in our time of need. Volunteer crews from many states helped rebuild the electrical grid and slowly power came to many homes. Yet almost two months after the storm only 25% of the homes had electricity. It took more than 70 days for us to get power back in Ramey.

A very famous Spanish chef, Chef José Andrés, came to Puerto Rico just days after the storm and organized a large group of Puerto Rican chefs and cooks to work with his team and feed the people in need. They worked around the clock cooking up some really fine food so that thousands could enjoy at least one hot meal a day. In little over a month they made and distributed more than one million free meals working out of *el Choliseo*, Puerto Rico's number one colosseum. Eventually, they got food trucks, helicopters, boats and cars to take food to the people if they could not make it to where the cooks were. It was great to see so many people working so hard to help each other.

These volunteers also helped bring food and water to places like Utuado which was hit especially hard. There were groups of ex-veterans that moved to the area to clear roads and rescue people. There was even this one man who traveled all the way from Alaska to Utuado with his chainsaw and stayed in Puerto Rico for a whole month working hard to help others.

The more than 5 million Puerto Ricans living stateside sent tons of food, water, batteries and all kinds of supplies to help their families back home. They were called love packages and there were so many of them that the Post Office was overwhelmed for months by the amount of things that were sent to the island. My dear sister alone sent us six boxes full of food to help us get by. It was hard not to feel pride in the way so many good people from so many different places came together as one to help each other thru these very hard times.

Sadly, not everyone was at their best behavior during this terrible crisis and you need to know the whole story. In some parts of Puerto Rico crime became a very big problem. Since criminals knew that the communication grid was down and that most police officers were too busy working on the recovery effort they took advantage of the situation. In some places thieves broke into people's homes and stole whatever they could. Many families had small gas powered generators that kept some of their appliances working. These generators were a favorite target of the heartless bullies who would come in the night and take them away to sell them in the black market at incredibly high prices. The thieves also knew that since ATM and credit cards were useless most people carried cash. This made them bigger targets.

Some business owners displayed their dark side by overcharging people for essential things. Food, bottled water, candles, batteries were terribly overpriced but some buyers were desperate and would pay anything for these things. Fortunately in the era of smart phones most of these heartless business people ended up being identified by the people and punished by the government. Customers would take pictures of the overpriced items and the businesses that were breaking the law and give them to the authorities. When caught many paid a minimum fine of 10 thousand dollars.

These were just some of the things that were happening all around you when you were a baby. So remember, you Amaia survived the great hurricane of 2017 with your family in Puerto Rico.

We all survived because we did what good families do. We all stuck together and protected each other. Not even big bad María could break our will to move on and rebuild. Once María stopped destroying everything she found, we all got back on our feet and rebuilt not only houses and power grid. We rebuilt our lives.

We learned many things for Hurricane María. We learned to drink water at room temperature and be grateful that we had it. We learned to eat canned spaghettis from paper plates and also be happy we had them. We enjoyed more quite conversations and enjoyed each other's company more. With no TVs nor devices to distract us, we paid more attention to each other and that was a good thing.

Time seemed to move so much slower without all the things that usually distracted us away from each other. We also learned that we could live with far less material things than we thought possible. Those of us who were paying attention learned a new found gratitude for everything we once took for granted.

With very little artificial light we learned to look up at the night sky and be impressed by the millions of stars that were now so easy to see. You my dear would point your little finger up to the sky and say 'la moon'. Ha, ha, your first attempts at Spanglish. I will never forget those difficult yet special days that came after María violently knocked on our doors.

Yet perhaps the most important lesson we all learned from this terrible event was that *love beats storms*, all kinds of storms, *every single time*.

Your *Abuelo's* Four Lists:

I am sure that in time you will probably have your own lists of favorite books, songs and movies. What follows are just samples of some of the stuff that your grandfather loved. You may not like them all and that's fine. Check some of them out anyway.

I hope you enjoy them as much as I did. Most of them will be very old to you but in books, music and movies you may find that like fine wine, sometimes the older they are the better they are. There's a reason why most of these movies, books and songs are still very popular decades after the first came out.

Movies:

1. It's a Wonderful Life (1943)
2. The Wizard of Oz (1939)
3. Twelve Angry Men (1957)
4. The Notebook (2004)
5. The Princess Bride (1987)
6. Back to the Future (The Trilogy)
7. Star Wars Movies: (Original Trilogy) A New Hope, Return of the Jedi, The Empire Strikes Back
8. ET The Extraterrestrial (1982)
9. Jurassic Park (1993)
10. Inside Out (2015)
11. Jurassic World (2015)
12. Wonder Woman (2017)
13. Up (2009) Disney animated classic
14. WALL-E (2008)
15. Toy Story (all four movies)

16.The Little Mermaid (1989)

Books:

1. Seven Habits of Highly Effective Teens, Sean Covey
2. Rich Dad Poor Dad, Robert Kiyosaki
3. The Little Prince, Antoine de Saint-Exupery
4. Animal Farm, George Orwell
5. From Me to We, Craig and Marc Kielburger
6. Outliers, Malcolm Gladwell
7. Cosmos, Carl Sagan
8. The Demon Haunted World, Carl Sagan
9. Chasing the Scream, Johann Hari
10.A Puerto Rican in New York, Jesús Colón
11.Tropical Tales of Terror, Roberto Guzmán-Sosa
12. Cosmos, Carl Sagan

Notable TED Talks:

1. A Girl who demanded a School, Kakenya Ntaiya
2. How to be a Person, Shane Koyczan
3. Why do we Sleep?, Russell Foster

4. What happens when you lose everything?, David Hoffman

5. What defines Me?, Lizzie Velasquez

6. Teaching English without Teaching English, Roberto Guzmán, TED X UPR

7. Does Money make you mean?, Paul Piff

8. My daughter Malala, Ziauddin Yousafzai

9. Save the Oceans, feed the World, Jackie Savitz

10. Are you sure about that? Think again, Roberto Guzmán, TED X UPR

11. Everything you think about addiction is wrong, Johann Hari

Music:

1. Hello Goodbye, The Beatles

2. Yellow Submarine, The Beatles

3. What a Wonderful World, Louis Armstrong, Sam Cooke

4. Feels so Good, Chuck Mangione

5. Don't Know much about History, Sam Cooke

6. My Girl, The Temptations

7. Side Show, Blue Magic

8. Stand by Me, Play for Change

9. Time in a Bottle, Jim Croce

10. Bohemian Rhapsody, Queen

11. Time after Time, Cindy Lauper
12. Somewhere Over the Rainbow, Judy Garland, Isreal "IZ" Kamakawiwo'ole
13. Rhapsody in Blue, George Gershwin
14. An American in Paris, George Gershwin
15. Que Será, José Feliciano
16. Light my Fire, The Doors, José Feliciano
17. Buscando America, Rubén Blades y Seis del Solar
18. El Padre Antonio y el Monaguillo Andrés, Rubén Blades y Seis del Solar
19. Boricua en la Luna, Roy Brown
20. Ayuburi, Roy Brown
21. En la Vida todo es Ir, Haciendo Punto en Otro Son
22. Verde Luz, Antonio Cabán Vale
23. Oubao Moin, Haciendo Punto en Otro Son
24. Cantar es Vivir, Haciendo Punto en Otro Son
25. Vida Campesina, Haciendo Punto en Otro Son
26. Grandes Éxitos, Juan Luis Guerra y 440

Dance Videos:

1. Singing in the Rain, Gene Kelly
2. Stormy Weather, the Nicholas Brothers (1943)

3. The Tap Awakens, Post Modern Jukebox, Sarah Reich
4. Umbrella-Vintage "Singing in the Rain" Casey Abrams and the Sole Sisters
5. Thriller, Michael Jackson
6. Evolution of Tap Dance, Post Modern Jukebox and Sarah Reich

About Politics

"Diapers and politicians should be changed often, both for the same reasons."

Anonymous

"Anyone who says they are not interested in politics is like a drowning man who insists he is not interested in water."

Mahatma Gandhi

Every day of our lives we need to get things done. We need to eat, drink and have shelter. We need places where we can be safe to work, to rest, to live and to enjoy life with the ones we love. Good neighborhoods, nice parks and comfortable homes are things we all need. If we get sick we may need medical care and maybe a place like a hospital where others can help us get well again.

All these needs are better served if people get together and form different groups to help each other. The smallest and perhaps the most important group is the family. There are many different kinds of families. Some have a mom and a dad who take care for each other and their own children, their little ones. Others may have only a mom or only a dad. Sometimes grandparents must take care of their grandchildren. In the early 20th century extended families were very common. In Puerto Rico whole barrios were often known by the name of only one family because most of the homes there belonged to a large family with many uncles, aunts, cousins and grandparents living in clusters of houses all near each other. Names like *Sector Acevedo, Sector Ruiz* or *Sector Guzmán* were all very common.

Some families are small while others are big. Most families, however, have some things in common. The members may be connected by blood. You, my dear, are a part of your mom and dad. You exist because they existed before you. This is the biological connection. You came from them the same way I came from my own parents.

The other bond that holds all good families together is love. Love allows people to work together to take care of each other. A baby cannot take care of herself. She needs others to do it for her. That's why you should be very grateful that you have so many people who love you and will do all they can to protect and help you. Some families are not physically related to each other but if there is love there is no need for that blood connection, they are without question a family because they are bonded by love.

The family however is not the only group humans have created to get things done. People also have sports groups, church groups and many other groups they join to take part in activities they enjoy. You may, for example, join other young people to do sports, or learn martial arts or learn how to play a musical instrument. That's how people get important things done. That's also how people make new friends.

Things are so much easier when we all help each other. One way we do this is by creating rules. Rules give us organization and *organization gives us freedom* and maybe even happiness. When people are organized they save time, effort and resources. Things get done faster, with less work and better results.

For example, your mom will give you rules that will protect you from harm. She may set a specific hour for bedtime so that you can get enough rest for the next day. You may not like all her rules but you need to trust her and follow them. In the case of bedtime, we know that good rest is essential for a good life. People who do not sleep enough are more likely to be grumpy, get sick and feel tired all day long.

Well, just as a family needs good rules to protect itself, society also needs some rules to work properly for the greater good of everybody. Traffic rules or laws are good examples. Red lights mean stop. Green lights mean go. If you're driving a car in the US or Puerto Rico you stay on the right side of the road. That way people driving in the opposite direction will not crash with you. By following these rules or laws we can all move from point A to point B safely and quickly.

Politics are supposed to work the very same way as smaller groups do. People get together and form this thing called a government. The government is made up of individuals who are chosen to protect and promote the things that everyday people, like you and me, need. This is called *democracy, a government that is chosen by the people to represent the needs and interests of the people.* For this we have elections where citizens vote for the best representatives they can find.

There are many different positions in a representative democracy. We have mayors who represent and rule the people of a small town like Saint Cloud, Aguadilla or Kissimmee, or even a big city, like New York, Dallas or Miami. We have governors who oversee a whole state like Florida, New York or even Puerto Rico. Finally, in the US we have a president who rules over all 50 states and territories like Puerto Rico.

All these positions exist to help us all build and maintain good roads, good bridges and good schools. When we have good mayors, good governors and a good president, things work well, good things get done.

The problem is that the people who are in public positions are not always smart or good. Sometimes they do not represent the people at all. They only work for themselves and those who pay them. That is why it is important to be aware of what is happening in politics. Some politicians may even create laws or adopt practices that end up hurting the people they were elected to protect and serve.

How do you tell a good politician from a bad one? Just listen to what they say then look at what they do. At the end of the day *it's their actions* that count the most. So, read the papers, listen to the politicians on social media and follow the issues that affect you and those around you. See if they help most of the people and protect our planet's resources, its water, air and land. We only have one Earth and we need to take care of it.

Make politics a topic you know about so that you can support those politicians who best work for you. Hold them accountable and learn as much as you can about the decisions that affect you and society in general. Once you do this you can decide to what degree you want to get involved in the process itself. Who knows? Maybe someday you can become a mayor, a governor or maybe even president.

You need to look at *three areas* when learning about your government. These are the *legislature*, the *executive* and the *judicial* branches. The first part, the legislature, is the group of people that make the rules or laws that all citizens are supposed to live by. It is called Congress at the federal level and *El Capitolio* in Puerto Rico.

The second part, the executive, is the one that makes sure people follow the laws created by the legislature. The police department, public roads, the school system and hospitals are all administered by the executive. The mayors, governors and the president are all part of the executive branch.

Finally, the judicial system is the part of the government that explains the laws whenever these are not clear for the people or the government. These are the courts that we have all over the country. If people are accused of breaking the law this is where they are taken first, to a court where a person called a *judge* decides if they in fact did anything wrong. The judged often has the help of others in deciding. These other people are the *jury*, a group that is made up of twelve regular citizens. If the person is found guilty then the courts decide what the appropriate punishment is.

As a responsible person it is always good for you to be informed of what all these people are doing and how it affects, for good or bad, others. Thomas Jefferson, one of the country's early presidents, once said that for democracy to work it needs *an informed citizenry*. People need to know what's going on so that they can participate in the *decision making process* and protect themselves from dishonest politicians.

Concentrate on two things. First, look at the politician's record of public service. How long has she been around? What has she done FOR THE PEOPLE she represents? If you like what you see maybe you should consider lending her your support and vote. Then look at her *platform*. The platform is the list of things she promises to do if elected.

All candidates have a plan that they promise to put into place if they are elected. If the politician is running for re-election then you have a good point of reference. Did this person keep her previous promises? Or did she turn her back on what she said once she was elected? If she did, you know she is not trustworthy, so beware.

So, in a nutshell, we have politics because they help us organize effectively into groups to solve problems, to get things done. That's what your *abuelo* thinks. I will not tell you what to believe. However, I will give you a small piece of advice. When deciding who to vote for do not focus on the name or the looks of a candidate. Do not worry too much about labels or slogans. Always focus on what people actually do.

About being a Teen

"Why fit in when you were born to stand out?"

Dr. Seuss

As you will surely discover, being a teen, (ages 13 to about 19) will not always be easy. These are the years when you slowly stop being a child and will become a young adult. For a few years it may feel like you're caught in the middle of childhood and adulthood, in a virtual twilight zone. Things will be different. Your body may feel strange and changing. You may not always like what you see in the mirror but hang in there. Things will get better. Your issues will not be only with yourself. They may involve how you see others, particularly your own family. There's a very good chance that you may feel most adults are hopelessly out of touch and old fashioned, like they don't really know what you're going thru and who you are.

There are a few important things you should know about being a teen. Of course, there have always been teenagers, but the fact of the matter is that teenagers *as we know them today* have only existed for less than a century. All the way up to the 1930s American society was divided into adults and children. People between the ages of 13 and 19 were *not considered a separate group* or demographic. They were never segregated nor did they spend much time interacting amongst themselves. Girls spent most of their time with adult women and boys spent most of their time with adult men. That's how they learned what society expected of them in terms of values and behavior. This was also true in most countries all over the planet.

After World War II, in the 1940s, all that changed. The easy availability of public schools, often even cars, and changing expectations all combined to form a new, a separate social group. Now, for the first time, teens were seen as a separate group. All this also created a new set of problems for all those involved.

For instance, the separation of teens into groups with people of their same age, made them more vulnerable to all kinds of trouble. While previous generations depended on experienced adults to help them solve problems and mature socially, many modern day teens go to other youngsters that are often just as lost and confused as they are. So the proverbial blind are often leading the blind.

Thus, many young people turn to pop-culture in search of guidance. Singers, athletes and actors are often the main role models that some try to emulate. This is probably not always a good idea. Why? Well, a person's skills as an athlete says nothing about her character or values. Other than a strong work ethic and physical aptitude there's very little we can know about a person by his talent as a basketball, baseball or soccer player. Nada.

The same can be said of a talented singer. With actors it can get even more difficult. Actors are people who make a living pretending to be someone else. What can we really know about their values from their talent as professional pretenders? Again, nothing. Doesn't it make more sense to admire and imitate people who are important and good at being themselves?

Society rewards the most successful of these people with fabulous fame and fortune and millions of people, particularly teens, imitate them and see them as role-models. They are often even seen as *heroes*. Heroes they are not. They are simply *celebrities*. They are people that are highly talented in one very specific area and for this they are recognized and celebrated. However, we should never blindly adopt them as our role models.

Another common problem is that teens have become a favorite target of profit seeking marketers, people that want to sell them something. As teens have more money at their disposal, those who want to take that money away from them promote their products more aggressively.

Many marketers will try to make teens believe that if they don't dress in a certain way, or have a certain cell-phone or listen to a particular kind of music they will not be accepted in this or that group. At my campus I've seen fashions come and go. It is amusing, to say the least, to see so many young people striving to be 'original' by dressing exactly the same way their friends do. Strange, ha ha.

The late teen years may often be the time of first love. What can I tell you about this? Well, for starters *do not rush it*. There is no need to 'be' with anybody else until you *first learn how to be with yourself.*

Concentrate on becoming a full grown woman before becoming someone's girlfriend. Enjoy the freedom of being able to travel wherever you want to go. Invest time and work in building yourself up first. Become the best Amaia you can possibly be. This often means using your resources, *you time, effort, money and mental skills* in becoming an adult.

This is how it works Amaia. A spoon, a shovel or a hammer rarely breakdown. That's because they're simple machines, one or two parts. A car or an airplane has thousands of parts that can at any given moment fail, sometimes with awful consequences.

Life is very much like that. *The fewer parts it has, the easier it is to maintain* and the harder it is to break. The more relationships you have the more likely it is for things to go wrong. Many romantic relationships are high maintenance. They tend to consume a lot of time, effort, money and emotions. The trouble is that you probably have a lot of other things going on in your life which will compete for these same things.

Now you have to decide what come first, your priorities. *If you are not very careful you may end up sacrificing things that are most important to do things that are really less valuable.* Don't commit to something that big too early in life. Chances are you don't really need to, so you shouldn't really want it.

The first time a person falls in love may seem like an almost magical experience. You may feel that that other person is just perfect. You may feel that you cannot live without that significant other. Sorry to disappoint you but *that is simply not true.*

You were a complete young woman BEFORE you meet that person and you'll continue to be complete AFTER that person is gone. Maybe you will cry or feel terrible after a breakup but trust me, you will survive and after a while it won't even matter why you broke up or fell out of love. *La vida continúa.* Don't you ever forget that my dear Amaia.

To complicate things even more, many parents are often too busy making a living outside of the home to really be there to help their struggling teens. But before you feel too judgmental remember, modern society is often very hard on working mothers by *demanding that they raise their children like they don't have jobs and at the same time expect them to hold jobs like they don't have children.* (I hate the term *working* mothers because ALL mothers are working mothers, especially those who stay home raising a family full time.) So, be patient with your family. They are probably doing the best they can but as you already know, they are far from perfect.

This, however doesn't mean that you should keep them in the dark when it comes to your life, your wants and needs. Your family loves you and you should always let them know when you need help. As I explained earlier, isolation is NEVER a good idea. So never isolate yourself or allow others to do it to you.

Oddly, the word for teenager in Spanish is very telling. It's *adolocente*, one who is in pain. Transitions are, generally speaking, very painful things because most people do not like change very much. Most of us want nice, stable lives. In the case of teenagers, these changes are often big and life changing. Everything, your body, your mind, your social settings and relationships are all in flux. That's the bad news. The good news is that to a great degree you can control many of these changes. Well, so much for the history lesson.

Here is some specific advice on how to survive or even thrive in those challenging teen years, eight things you need to know now.

- Understand that the changes you are going thru are *completely normal* and they are *for your benefit*. They are how you grow into adulthood.

- *Do not limit yourself* to other teens for companionship and advice. Your mom and other *loving, responsible adults* should always be among those you share your life and thoughts with.

- Always *focus on your personal growth* and development. *Join other like-minded young people.* Good friends are very important.

- Remember, *you are not the center of the universe*. Most of the problems you face will be the same millions of others have faced before you. Find out how others dealt with their challenges. This means that *there are plenty of people who understand perfectly well what you are going thru* so listen up. Learn from those people in your times of trouble.

- *Never*, ever, *isolate yourself for a long time* when you are sad or in trouble. We humans are social creatures. We need others to survive and prosper.

Find people, young and old, you can trust and ask for help when in need.

- *Keep busy*. Fill your life with meaningful activities. Do sports. Play an instrument. Help others. Busy people don't have time for feeling depressed or lonely. Life is like riding a bike. If you stop moving you will fall to the side. Do not waste your time staring at a screen. Girl, as I said before, your body was meant for moving so keep active.

- Always remember, *you do not need to fit in* with anybody to be happy. You do not need to belong to any particular group to be successful. The peer pressure to belong is often very strong. *Never let others define you.* You are you and if someone doesn't like you that's their problem not yours.

- Finally, *be grateful* for all that is good in your life. Gratitude cannot co-exist with greed because when you value and love what is good in your life you stop focusing on what is bad.

Being a teenager will not always be easy but if done right it can be one of the best times of your life. Just hold on tight and enjoy the ride.

About caring for a Broken Heart:

"Only time can heal a broken heart as only time can heal a broken leg."

Miss. Piggy

"New beginnings are often disguised as painful endings."

Lao Tzu

Sorry to say this but your heart will one day feel broken. It happens to everybody and it will probably happen to you. You will feel terrible, and lost and very sad. You will cry. You may feel so bad that you'll think the world is about to end. Perhaps you found out that somebody you trusted betrayed you. You really thought this person was your friend but he really wasn't.

Life can be very unpredictable and hard. Sadly, people and things change. You may even feel so bad sometimes that you will think there is no way out. That's the bad news Amaia.

The good news is that the world won't end. Both the world and you will survive. A broken heart is a terrible thing to suffer but it is also an inevitable part of living. When things do not go our way we often wonder why. Maybe the broken heart is the product of a breakup. What do you do when you have fallen in love with someone and that other person doesn't feel the same way? Will you ever find happiness without that one 'super special' person? That 'perfect' person?

The first thing you need to remember is *that happiness is not something somebody else can give you.* You do not need any particular person or thing to be happy. It is never outside you. Happiness comes from *within* you. *It's not so much what happens to you that makes you happy as to how you react to whatever happens.* Some people complain about rainy days. Others go out and enjoy the shower and jump and splash in the puddles.

However, the great irony is that knowing this will not in itself make you feel any better, because sadness is never about knowing. Sadness is always about feelings.

The truth is that feelings are a big part of being a person, being human. These bad moments define us and even when they seem to be hurting us we need to *acknowledge* them. Accepting them doesn't mean that they're always OK. If I fall and I break an arm I must accept the fact that I have a broken arm. It's a freaking painful fact but pretending it didn't happen isn't going to do me any good. I will seek medical attention and maybe the doctor will put my arm in a cast for a few weeks. It will feel bad for a while but eventually the cast will be removed and I will feel so much better.

There are some things that you can do to deal with this extreme sadness. First, keep busy. Sadness hates a moving target. Take time to *be with others* that encourage and support you. *Do exercise* or *begin a new project* you wanted to do but didn't have the time for. Were you thinking about *learning something* new? A new sport or playing a musical instrument perhaps? Now is the time. You will *meet new people* as you learn new skills and enjoy yourself. Remember, *you were a complete, wonderful person before this experience and you will continue to be a complete and wonderful person after this bad experience.*

The one thing you should NEVER do is to isolate yourself. Disconnecting yourself from the things and people you love is NEVER a good idea. Isolation leads to loneliness and that can make your broken heart even more so.

The second thing you should do is realize that there is *nothing wrong with asking others for help.* In fact, no one will know what's going on unless you tell them. Of course, this doesn't mean you're going to put your personal life on public exhibition for the world to see on social media.

Your pain is a private matter not a reality show. Your personal life is not for the casual entertainment of others who don't really care about you. Don't put everything that happens to you on Facebook or social media. Only those that need to know should know. Share your sadness only with people who truly care about you and can be trusted.

The third thing you can do is *make some changes* in your habits and surroundings. Get rid of the things that remind you of whatever is causing you pain. If it was a breakup, then stop going to the places you used to visit together for a while. Don't listen to that song you two shared. If you two had specific things that you did together then change those activities for new ones. Focus on the now, not the past. Remember what I told you earlier.

The past is a place of reference not residence. Learn from this pain and how it happened so you don't make the same mistakes again. Remember, you have your whole life to make new, interesting and brand new mistakes... Ha ha ha...

Sometimes heartbreak comes with company. It brings along two very evil twins, anger and fear. These two can destroy you if you let them. You are angry because things did not work out the way you expected them to. You are fearful of moving on because you think it's going to happen again and you may feel you are not strong or smart enough to succeed in the future. All that is nonsense.

So, how do you deal with anger? Easy, look at all the *good* things in your life. Think about your loved ones, your possessions and all the many things you still have that others only dream about. You cannot be grateful and angry at the same time. *Gratitude is one of the most important feelings anyone can ever have.*

When you value what you already have you realize that perhaps things are not as bad as they may seem at first. So *appreciate all your blessings* and slowly but surely your heart will mend.

Fear, anger's evil twin, can also be a big problem. If you let it take control of you, fear will stop you from moving on and getting over your bad experiences. Fear can paralyze a person to the point where she will not even try some things again. Thinker Robin Sharma put it nicely when he wrote: "The fears we don't face become our limits." That's why we must never ignore our fears. Acknowledge them and confront them.

Keep in mind that *failing is how we learn new things in life*. If you let fear stop you, you will never achieve your goals or dreams. Someone once said that when the going gets tough, the tough get going. A bit of a cliché there, but truthful none the less.

That is how you deal with a broken heart. You accept your pain and you work towards learning from it. You get going with your life and you stay in touch with the things and people that matter to you. You are stronger than you think and you will overcome the challenges that life will throw your way.

There's an old song by Jamaican singer Pato Banton. You may want to check it out. It's titled "Never Give In". Catchy little tune. This simple song has some great advice on never giving in when faced with challenges.

About saying Goodbye:

"Do not be sad because it ended. Be happy because it happened."

Dr. Seuss

"Life is a series of hellos and goodbyes. I'm afraid it's time for goodbye again."

Billy Joel

"You say yes, I say no, you why and I say I don't know. You say goodbye and I say hello..."

The Beatles

My dear Amaia, one of the most difficult things we must all do in life is to say goodbye. Many people will come into our lives but most of them will not stay for long. We may want them to stay but many just won't. Sometimes they simply have other plans that may not include us. Sometimes it's us who want to move away or end a relationship.

And sometimes people just pass away, they die. I remember when my dad past away. It was not a complete surprise. He was 75 years old and he was not in very good health. His heart was weak and one day it simply stopped beating. He was working on one of his cars, washing it I think. He felt a strong pain in his chest and he collapsed next to the car. Mom saw him and immediately knew something was terribly wrong. She asked some neighbors for help but it was too late. When the paramedics came he was gone, he had died. Mom called me and I rushed to their side. That was one of the saddest days of my life.

Many years later I still miss him terribly. But dad was not my only very difficult goodbye. As you may know I wasn't very good at romantic relationships. I divorced three times. Each time I thought that this was going to be the love of my life. It did not turn out that way. We said goodbye. Sometimes goodbyes make you sad and may even make you cry.

Nothing wrong with that. Cry if you must. Do not deny your feelings. *Feeling sad is just as natural as feeling happy.* Just one more feeling of the many feelings you will have as you grow up. But life went on for me as it will go on for you. In time I had other wonderful things to live for, my family, my career, my writing and most recently getting to meet you.

There are a few things that you should remember when parting ways. *Never assume that someone is leaving because there is something wrong with you.* NEVER. There are many things involved in breakups and no one can control them. People and their feelings are very complicated. Often, not even the person himself knows why he's doing some things.

Sometimes people separate because their goals in life are different and they need to be in different places. Sometimes they simply love different things or activities in life. For instance, a person who just loves to read and visit libraries and museums probably shouldn't be with someone who cannot let a weekend go by without going to a party, the beach and go out bar hopping.

A deeply religious person probably shouldn't pair with a non-believer or an atheist. Life and circumstance can also come between people and that does not mean that either of them is bad. *They are just different.* Letting people go may not be easy but it is often inevitable. We cannot force ourselves to love someone and by the same token we cannot force anyone to love us.

Please keep in mind that *hugs and kisses can never be forced. They are only valuable if they are given freely, openly and lovingly.* Accepting this will liberate you from depending on others for your own happiness. The pain of the unwanted goodbye will fade away with time and you will find satisfaction and happiness with other people, experiences and things.

If it's a romantic rejection don't you ever forget that you should never beg anybody for their love and affection. *Ni el amor ni la amistad se mendigan.* I repeat, you should *never* beg anyone for either love or friendship. If someone does not appreciate you for what you are worth, it is their loss. So never be afraid of letting go when necessary.

You always need to be a good listener. Most people aren't. An unanswered message is in itself an answer. When a person does not pick up your calls they may be telling you they are not interested without saying a single word. So *listen to the silences as carefully as you listen to words.*

Once people become beggars they loss their self-respect and their dignity. Never, ever do that my dear. Cry in private if you must but never forget that there will always be another tomorrow.

Life is a dance that will take twists and turns constantly, enjoy the music and be grateful for all the good things and good moments that come your way but do not become overly attached to anything or anyone. Having good memories is a wonderful thing. Take pictures, write diaries, and keep records of your adventures. *Enjoy every today for soon it will become a yesterday*. Do not worry too much about tomorrow because no one really knows how many of those they will ever have.

About Growing Old:

"Aging is the process by which we become the person we were always meant to be."

David Bowie

I have no way of knowing what your world's attitude towards aging will be but I do know my world. My world was obsessed with youth, beauty and health. The media was always showing beautiful, young and healthy people doing all sorts of great things. Marketing was often built around these three groups, the young, the attractive and the healthy to sell us all kinds of things. They wanted us to believe that if we used whatever they were selling we too would be part of the 'beautiful' people. This was, of course, a very big lie. No one needs to look in any specific way or be of a certain age to be a beautiful person.

With very few exceptions the old, the average looking and the not so healthy were almost never seen. If you watch, God forbid, ha, ha, *telenovelas*, Hispanic soap operas, almost everybody is painfully beautiful. Everybody except the bad guys that is. Turn down the volume of a still telenovela you've never seen before and watch it for ten minutes. Try to guess who the good guys and the bad guys are. Turn up the volume and watch for another ten minutes and if you're smart you probably guessed that the good guys were usually the attractive actors while the unattractive characters were the bad guys.

You'd think that almost everybody in the countries that make these *telenovelas* is under the age of forty, in top physical shape and terribly sexy.

The trouble in real life is that those three attributes do not last. So even if you do happen to be young, pretty and healthy that's not going to last forever.

I am sorry to say, but you will grow old and if looks and health are all you have going for you,

you're in for a big disappointment. Slowly but surely there will be lines on your face and you will get a bit slower and you may even gain some weight. You can slow down the aging process if you eat right, exercise and take care of yourself but you can never stop it.

But that's all right. That too is part of life. As British singer David Bowie said, aging can be a wonderful thing. It can help you become the person you always should have been. So if you do things right you may not be getting more beautiful on the outside but on the inside you may be becoming the most beautiful person imaginable.

And that inner beauty may be more important than most people think. Being externally attractive is nice but it is not enough. If there is no content, no significant character, or values *there will be nothing left once youth has passed*. The obsession that my society had with these three things is a denial of reality and it promoted very bad attitudes. It made people aspire to unrealistic goals. It made them very *superficial*.

You do not have to look like a super-model to be attractive. The looks that are often mindlessly promoted by the media make everyday people think that they are not beautiful enough or young enough. That is nonsense. I'll let you in on a little secret. Not even the models themselves look like the girls and guys you see every day in those ads. There's this thing called photo-shop that people use to digitally change the pictures of the models and by the time they've reached your tablet's screen they've been changed around so much that not even the model can recognize herself anymore.

To deny aging is to deny life and reality. Growing old is not a bad thing when you realize that, like everything else in life, it all depends on what you do with it. As people grow older they learn to value things that they may have overlooked earlier in life. They realize how important the 'little' things are. The smile of a child, a good book, a lovely sunset or a family get-together become more important. Things that before seemed insignificant suddenly become very important.

Sometimes even getting sick can be a good thing. When I had my heart attack I realized how important my family was to me. Having stuff just wasn't that important to me anymore. I rediscovered the value of conversation and the enjoyment of music. I learned how to slow down a bit and savor the details of everyday living. I was slowly becoming the man I always wanted to be as Bowie so eloquently said.

This is one issue you need not worry about any time soon. It will be decades before you start to grow old. But it will happen so know that it's not bad at all. We are all much more than our physical bodies or our age. Even in bad health we are still valuable and our lives are still important.

Do not be obsessed with your looks or your age. Focus instead of staying young in your mind and heart. Find friends that understand this too, people that love you for who you are not what you look like.

About Time:

"Your time is limited so don't waste it living some else's life."

Steve Jobs

"Happily ever after doesn't mean forever. It just means time, a little time."

River Song from Doctor Who

You can replace a lot of things in life. If you lose your keys you can get new copies made. If your car is stolen you can save up money and eventually get another one. Time, on the other hand, cannot be replaced. *Time is the stuff of life itself.*

Thousands of years ago a famous Chinese thinker called Buddha said "The trouble is you think you have time." Most people do not realize that we do not know how much time we have. Most of the people that died yesterday probably had plans for today. Unfortunately today never came for them. This means that *we should always be good to each other*.

This is not to say that you should constantly be worried about dying or running out of time. Women of your generation will have a life span of well over 80 years. My mom was 81 years old and was in perfect health when you came to us, so you have very good genes. If you take care of yourself you are most likely going to live a long, healthy life.

What I mean is that if you love someone let them know how you feel *today*. If you want to achieve a goal start working on it *now*. Set up *specific* goals with *specific* dates. Someone once said that *a goal is a dream with a deadline*. That is not a bad idea. Don't waste your life thinking that *someday* you're going to do this or *someday* you're going to go there. For some people someday never comes. And even if you live to be a hundred years old you still may find that life is short. So stay busy.

As you may have noticed, *time has three dimensions, past, present and future*. It seems that if you find a good balance of these three points of view you can make the most of your life. Some say they just don't have time for this or that, that they're too busy.

Well, guess what. We all have exactly the same amount of time every day, about 24 hours, no more, no less. The one thing that changes from one person to another is how they choose to use those 24 hours. You can be the poorest or the richest woman on the planet and your days will be exactly the same as everybody else's.

Some very smart people have studied this thing called time and how to use it successfully and they have found some interesting things. One such person, Dr. Philip Zimbardo, gave a very interesting TED talk on this topic called 'The Psychology of Time'. Zimbardo explained that some people spend a lot of their NOW thinking about their PAST. They feel bad because of all the terrible things that happened to them before. This is not good. *Living in the past will paralyze you* and stop you from enjoying your present. The past is a place of reference not residence.

Others spend most of their NOW thinking about the FUTURE. This isn't very smart either. As we saw earlier, we don't know how much future any of us has. Still others only think about their NOW. They never reflect on their past to look at their experiences and learn from them. They do not plan or think about the future at all. This too can be a very, very serious mistake. Goals, *specific* goals, make life worth living. Plan your life in terms of what you want to learn, where you want to go and how you want to grow and serve others. Look for a balance between the three dimensions of time that works for you. *Plan for the future, learn from the past but live in the now.* Remember time is the stuff of life. It is by far our most valuable resource and once gone it is irreplaceable. So use your time wisely.

About ending this book

My dear girl, there is still so much more that I want to share with you and I truly hope you will never need this book to know of my love for you. When many people become aware that their time is coming to an end they often panic. Their minds and hearts are filled with regrets about not having spent enough time with the ones they loved. They're full of sadness because there were so many things they wanted to do and share but never found the time.

Writer Horace Mann put it very nicely. He said "Be ashamed to die until you have won some victory for humanity." But, what is a victory for humanity? I think that what Mann meant was that we need to help others in some way before we pass away. We need to leave the world a little bit better than what it was when we got here.

This victory is different for everyone. A good teacher helps others learn how to educate themselves and use language, knowledge and action as amazing tools for personal growth. A dedicated nurse or doctor literally saves the lives of others when their bodies are failing them.

A good mother protects her children every second they are together. She is a teacher, a guardian, a doctor, a nutritionist, a cook and many, many other things. That's what your mom does for you 24/7 all year long. So be *very* proud of mamá too.

An artist expresses the emotions of others in music, dance, theater, paintings or literature. A skilled mechanic can make a car safe for a family to travel in, for food and services to be rendered to others in trucks and vans. All these people have one thing in common. They are all achieving in their own special way victories for other people, victories for humanity.

We all seek to help ourselves in life and that's fine but that should never be enough. We must also strive to help others. It's called *a legacy*, what we wish to leave behind once we are gone. When you grow a bit older, perhaps age 13, I encourage you to listen to a wonderful poem by a young man called Shane Koyczan. Its title is *How to be a Person*. We have been given a life and we should treasure that special gift we have been granted. If used correctly, life can be a truly wonderful thing.

Even though I hope I can live to be a hundred years old I am not ashamed of dying anymore. That heart attack turned out to be a very good thing. It made me aware of the urgent need to do what needed to done before my time was up.

I realized that I needed to secure my legacy. Now I know that I have one. I have my two wonderful children, your mom Jenny and your uncle Kevin. When they were young I made mistakes as a father but I did my best to fix those mistakes the moment I realized I was wrong. For that I am sorry.

I also had the wonderful opportunity of meeting you, my amazing granddaughter. The joy that your presence meant for all of us, your *familia,* is beyond words. *You will always live in me as I will always live in you.*

I have a legacy in my books, especially this one, which will hopefully speak to others long after I am gone. Finally, I have a legacy in all the students I had the honor of serving during nearly 25 years at UPR Aguadilla. So I guess that when I die I need not feel ashamed for I did my best to leave the world a little bit better than I found it.

Now my little one, build your own legacy and as a Vulcan friend of mine once said, "Live long and prosper." TQM ;-) SIEMPRE... (I LOVE YOU VERY MUCH... ;-) ALWAYS)

About the Author

Roberto Guzmán-Sosa is a full professor at the University of Puerto Rico, Aguadilla Campus. He has worked there for many years teaching undergraduate English courses that range from Basic English classes to grammar and composition courses.

As a free-lance writer his books include a sci-fi fantasy short story collection titled *Tropical Tales of Terror*. The book *Mitos y Conflictos en la Biblia* is a commentary on the Scriptures from an agnostic perspective and *Heroes* is a collection of short essays celebrating the lives of outstanding individuals who are not as well-known as Roberto thinks they should be. In this book he discusses the differences between celebrities and heroes which he feels far too many people today confuse. Roberto was also the keynote speaker for the *Florida Literacy Conference* on May 10-12, 2017.

In late 2016 and early 2017 Roberto became a two times TED Talk speaker. His first talk was at UPR Mayaguez Campus and is titled *Teaching English without Teaching English* and his second talk was at the UPR Rio Piedras Campus and is titled *Are you Sure about that? Think Again*. Both can be seen on YouTube.

Roberto lives in the North-Western coast of Puerto Rico with his family and Molly the cat, an honorary member of the Guzmán family.

Títulos publicados:

El hombre del tiempo ángel m. agosto

Lustro de gloria ángel m. agosto

Intrigas desesperadas ángel m. agosto

Rutina rota ángel m. agosto

5 ensayos para épocas de revolución ángel m. agosto

Voces de bronce ángel m. agosto

Horror blanco ángel m. agosto

Relatos por voces diversas Cómplices en la palabra

Déjame decirte algo Cómplices en la palabra

En los límites Evaluz Rivera Hance

Lo que dice el corazón Evaluz Rivera Hance

Transversándome José Enrique García Oquendo

Emociones, versos y narrativa Grupo Cultural La Ceiba

El proceso político en Puerto Rico ángel m. agosto

ANA, auténtica forjadora de valor Ana Rivera

Angustia de amar Ana Rivera

Sindicalismo en tiempos borrascosos Radamés Acosta

Desde la sombra la luz William Morales Correa

Tinto de verano Anamín Santiago

Caroba Juan de Matta García

La brújula de los pájaros José Ernesto Delgado Carrasquillo

Esperaré en mi país invisible Mariela Cruz

Mancha de plátano Mariela Cruz

Loíza, desde El Ancón a tu Corazón Madreselvas de Puerto Rico

Los molinos de doña Elvira Luccía Reverón

Un vistazo a la tierra de los mil dioses Armando Casas Macías

Oscar hecho en poesía Poetas en Marcha

Soy un millar de vientos ángel m. agosto

25 de julio Roberto Tirado

En mi vientre oscuro Anamín Santiago

Del MPI al PSP, el eslabón pedido ángel m. agosto

Teatro oculto en "La Sataniada" de Alejandro Tapia y Rivera Anamín Santiago

Años de fuego, periodismo de combate (1971-76) ángel m. agosto

Abuela Itzé Norma Medina Carrillo

La abuela asesina Yván Silén

Me quedo con las mujeres Juan González-Bonilla

Juan Mari Brás: ¿el estratega de la independencia? ¿El socialismo una consigna? ángel m. agosto

www.ingramcontent.com/pod-product-compliance
Lightning Source LLC
Chambersburg PA
CBHW061757250726
48657CB00001B/171